New Inside Out

Scan the CD at the

back of the book

Peter Maggs, Catherine Smith,
Jon Hird & Vaughan Jones

Elementary

Workbook

Macmillan Education
Between Towns Road, Oxford OX4 3PP
A division of Macmillan Publishers Limited
Companies and representatives throughout the world

ISBN 978-1-4050-8595-3 (with key edition)
ISBN 978-1-4050-8596-0 (without key edition)

Original design by Jackie Hill, 320 Design Limited
Page make-up by Carolyn Gibson
Illustrated by Phil Garner, Peter Harper, Ben Hasler and Ed McLachlan
Cover design by Andrew Oliver

Story 'The Canterville Ghost' retold by Stephen Colbourn (Macmillan Publishers Limited
2005), copyright © Stephen Colbourn 2005, reprinted by permission of the publisher.

Authors' acknowledgements
We would like to thank the New Inside Out team: Sue Kay and Vaughan Jones,
Desmond O'Sullivan, Rafael Alarcon-Gaeta, and our wonderful editor, Alyson Maskell.

The authors and publishers would like to thank the following for permission to
reproduce their photographs:
Alamy pp10(bl) Kyler Deutmeyer; 10(r) eStock Photo; 22 (l) Ben Walsh; 23 David Norton
Photos; 42 Picture Contact; 66(b) Peter Titmuss; 67 A Room with Views. BananaStock p16.
Corbis pp7; 12; 14(t); 18; 22(r); 24; 26; 31; 34; 35; 46; 47; 50; 62(tr), (bl), (br); 66(t), (c).
Empics pp14(cl); 28; 32. GettyImages p47(l). Ernst Hofmann, Hotel du Lac, Interlaken
p62(tl). Rex Features pp10(tl); 14(c), (cr), (bl), (br); 15; 27; 54. Catherine Smith pp11; 39.

Printed and bound in China

2011 2010 2009
10 9 8 7 6 5 4 3

Contents

1 Airport

Grammar

1 Complete the sentences with the verb *be*. Use contractions where possible.

a) A: Hello. I _'m___ Sandy. What _____ your name?

B: Hi, Sandy. I _am_ Danny. Nice to meet you.

b) A: Where _did_ she from?

B: She __IS__ from Russia.

c) A: _Are_ they Brazilian?

B: No, they _are_. They're Spanish.

d) A: _Is_ he three?

B: No, he __IS__ two.

e) A: _Are_ we in Spain?

B: No, I think we _are_ in Portugal.

2 Complete the sentences with *a* or *an*.

a) It's __a___ book.

b) It's _____ bag.

c) It's _____ umbrella.

d) It's _____ mobile phone.

e) It's _____ MP3 player.

f) It's _____ watch.

3 Complete the questions and answers.

a) What ___'s this_____ ?

___It's__ a key.

b) What ____are these____ ?

They're sweets.

c) What _____ ?

_____ a diary.

d) What _____ ?

_____ pens.

e) What _____ ?

_____ a coin.

f) What _____ ?

_____ aspirins.

g) What _____ ?

_____ magazines.

4 Put the words in order to make questions.

a) number   phone   What's   your   ?

_____

b) Are   British   you   ?

_____

c) email   What's   address   your   ?

_____

d) What's   bag   your   in   ?

_____

5 Write true answers to the questions in Exercise 4.

a) _____

b) _____

c) _____

d) _____

Vocabulary

1 Find seven countries and their languages in the wordsquare and complete the table below. Look → and ↓ .

A	J	C	H	I	N	E	S	E	D
J	R	O	C	B	S	P	A	I	N
A	S	G	N	R	C	P	F	R	S
P	O	E	I	A	H	O	O	P	A
A	T	R	A	P	I	L	I	A	N
N	R	M	I	I	N	A	T	J	I
E	U	A	O	L	A	N	A	A	R
S	S	N	N	M	G	D	L	P	U
E	S	Y	B	C	G	H	Y	A	S
W	I	T	A	L	I	A	N	N	S
I	A	S	P	A	N	I	S	H	I
P	O	L	I	S	H	A	F	D	A
D	S	N	G	E	R	M	A	N	N

Country	Language
China	Chinese

2 Write the numbers in words.

1 ___one___   **6** _____

2 _____   **7** _____

3 _____   **8** _____

4 _____   **9** _____

5 _____   **10** _____

3 Label the pictures (*a–l*) with the words in the box.

aspirins   book   camera   coin   diary
magazine   mobile phone   sweets   tissues
toothbrush   umbrella   watch

a) ____aspirins____   g) _____
b) _____   h) _____
c) _____   i) _____
d) _____   j) _____
e) _____   k) _____
f) _____   l) _____

4 Complete the conversation with the words in the box.

do   ~~How~~   repeat   Thanks

Student: (1) ___How___ do you say 'revista' in English?
Teacher: Magazine.
Student: How (2) _____ you spell it?
Teacher: M-A-G-A-Z-I-N-E. Magazine.
Student: Could you (3) _____ that, please?
Teacher: Sure. M-A-G-A-Z-I-N-E.
Student: OK. (4) _____ .

🔊 01 Listen and check.

Listening

1 🔘 02 **Cover the listening script. Listen to the conversation. Number the pictures 1–4 as you hear them.**

a

b

c Departures

d

Man:	And how do you spell your name?
Sonya:	S-O-N-Y-A.
Man:	And what's your telephone number?
Sonya:	0703 5268 401.
Man:	OK. Goodbye, Sonya. Phone me.
Sonya:	OK. Goodbye.
Beth:	Hi, Sonya. Mm, nice man. Is he American?
Sonya:	No, he's Spanish. He's from Madrid.
Beth:	What's his name?
Sonya:	Joaquin.
Beth:	How do you spell it?
Sonya:	J-O-A-Q-U-I-N.
Beth:	Oh ... Is this your bag?
Sonya:	Oh no! It's Joaquin's bag.
Beth:	What's in the bag?
Sonya:	A book, keys, ... mm and a diary!
Beth	Is his mobile phone in the bag?
Sonya:	No.
Beth:	What's his mobile number?
Sonya:	603 380230.
Beth:	Phone him.
Sonya:	603 380230. Hi, Joaquin. It's Sonya. Your bag's here.
Man:	Oh, thank you. Thank you.

2 **Listen again and <u>underline</u> the correct answer.**

a) The woman's name is **Carla** / <u>**Sonya**</u>.

b) The woman's telephone number is **0104 5268 441** / **0703 5268 401**.

c) The man's name is **Joaquin** / **Juan**.

d) The man is from **Spain** / **America**.

e) There's a **toothbrush** / **book** in his bag.

f) The man's mobile phone **is** / **isn't** in the bag.

g) The man's mobile number is **603 380230** / **603 388230**.

Pronunciation

1 🔘 03 **Listen and repeat the alphabet.**

A B C D   E F G   H I J K   L M N   O P Q
R S T   U V W   X Y Z

2 🔘 04 **Listen and number the abbreviations in the order you hear them.**

BBC	_____	UFO	_____
CIA	_____	UK	_____
CNN	_____	USA	_____
FBI	_____	VIP	_1_

Listen again and repeat.

Writing

Asian Air — VIP Card

Complete our form and win a flight to New York.

First name	Greg
Surname	White
Nationality	British
Home address	19 Joyce Street London England
Home phone number	00 44 208 432 448
Email address	gwhite@dubmail.com

Write two sentences to describe yourself.

I'm an English businessman. I'm from London.

1 Look at the VIP Card and tick (✓) the correct rules.

CAPITAL LETTERS

You always use a capital letter to

a) write first names ☐
b) write surnames ☐
c) write nationalities ☐
d) write street names ☐
e) write city names ☐
f) write country names ☐
g) write email addresses ☐
h) start sentences ☐

2 Write the sentences with capital letters. Remember to end each sentence with a full stop (.).

a) my name's katrina borkova

   My name's Katrina Borkova.

b) i'm from poland

   _____

c) i live in new york

   _____

d) my address is 42 madison avenue

   _____

e) my home phone number is 001 212 299 001

   _____

f) my email address is katrinab@info.com

   _____

3 Complete the VIP Card with your personal information.

Asian Air — VIP Card

Complete our form and win a flight to New York.

First name	
Surname	
Nationality	
Home address	
Home phone number	
Email address	

Write two sentences to describe yourself.

4 Write sentences like those in Exercise 2 about yourself. Use the information from your VIP Card.

Example

My name's Greg White. I'm from England.

_____

_____

_____

_____

_____

_____

2 People

Grammar

1 Complete the sentences with the words in the box.

her	His	Its	~~my~~	our	Their	your

a) I'm a writer. I love ___my___ job.

b) Nice to meet you. Is _____ name Jones?

c) She's French but _____ father is from Germany.

d) Is Paul here? _____ mother is on the phone.

e) It's a Persian cat. _____ name is Pushkin.

f) My wife and I are doctors but _____ son is an actor.

g) They're singers. _____ names are Fifi and Peach.

2 Write the words in order to make sentences.

a) this   pen   your   Is   ?
   Is this your pen?

b) favourite   actor   my   He's   .
   _____

c) Carla   Is   name   her   ?
   _____

d) Joe   with   friend   his   is   .
   _____

e) New York   is   from   teacher   Our   .
   _____

f) grandparents   Their   Arthur and Joan   are   .
   _____

3 Complete the table of the verb _be_: present simple.

	Affirmative	Negative
I		'm not
you	're	
he / she / it		
we		
they		

4 Complete the sentences with the affirmative of the verb _be_. Use contractions where possible.

a) I _'m___ from Poland.

b) My mother _____ a teacher.

c) My hairdresser _____ a man.

d) My favourite drink _____ tea.

e) My friends and I _____ students.

f) My grandparents _____ doctors.

5 Write the sentences from Exercise 4 in the negative.

a) _I'm not from Poland._____

b) _____

c) _____

d) _____

e) _____

f) _____

Tick (✓) the statements in Exercises 4 and 5 that are true for you.

6 Write questions.

a) you / an actor?
   Are you an actor?

b) your mother / over 50 years old?
   _____

c) your teacher / British?
   _____

d) your phone number / 01807 322 486?
   _____

e) your classmates / from Spain?
   _____

f) you and your family / from Russia?
   _____

7 Write true short answers to the questions in Exercise 6.

Example (a)

   No, I'm not.

a) _____

b) _____

c) _____

d) _____

e) _____

f) _____

Vocabulary

1 Find the words in the wordsnake.

actorfoodsportanimaldrinkwriterfilmsinger

a) _actor_   e) _____

b) _____   f) _____

c) _____   g) _____

d) _____   h) _____

2 Write an example of each word in Exercise 1.

a) _Harrison Ford_

b) _____

c) _____

d) _____

e) _____

f) _____

g) _____

h) _____

3 Write the numbers in full.

a) 16   _sixteen_

b) 21   _____

c) 46   _____

d) 73   _____

e) 115 _____

f) 312 _____

4 Write the sums in numbers and answer them.

a) fifteen + fifty =

   _15 + 50 = 65_

b) forty-five x ten =

   _____

c) twenty-nine – nineteen =

   _____

d) one hundred and thirteen + seventy-six =

   _____

e) three hundred and forty-five x two =

   _____

f) four hundred and sixty + two hundred and seventy-nine =

   _____

5 Look at the pictures and complete the crossword with the names of the jobs.

6 Complete the conversation with the words in the box.

| bad | How | Goodbye | meet | ~~morning~~ |
| Nice | See | this | well | you |

Jane: Hello, Harry.

Harry: Oh, good (1) ___morning___ , Jane.
        (2) _____ are you?

Jane: I'm very (3) _____ , thanks. And
        (4) _____ ?

Harry: Not too (5) _____ , thanks.

Jane: Harry, (6) _____ is Carol, my sister.

Harry: Nice to (7) _____ you, Carol.

Carol: (8) _____ to meet you, Harry.

Jane: OK. (9) _____ you, Harry.

Harry: Oh, yes. Bye, Jane. Bye, Carol.

Carol: (10) _____ , Harry.

🔊 05 Listen and check.

Reading

1 🔘 06 **Read the texts and match them with the photos.**

a) Photo _____

> Hi. My name's Elena Garcia. I'm 30 and I'm from Spain. I'm a lawyer. My favourite food is chips and my favourite singer is Bono from U2.

b) Photo _____

> Hello. I'm Bill Wiggins. I'm 55 and I'm from England. I'm married and I'm a taxi driver. My favourite singer is Frank Sinatra and my favourite drink is beer.

c) Photo _____

> Hi. My name's Aleksy Nowak. I'm 22 and I'm from Poland. I'm an IT technician. My favourite actor is Sean Connery and my favourite sport is football.

2 **Cover the texts. What do you remember about the people? Write the person's name.**

a) Age: 30

   Elena

b) Country: England

   _____

c) Favourite actor: Sean Connery

   _____

d) Favourite food: chips

   _____

e) Favourite drink: beer

   _____

f) Surname: Nowak

   _____

3 **Read the texts again. Answer the questions.**

a) What's Bill's surname?

   Wiggins

b) How old is Aleksy?

   _____

c) Is Bill married?

   _____

d) Where is Elena from?

   _____

e) Is Aleksy German?

   _____

f) Is Elena a hairdresser?

   _____

Writing

Using punctuation
Writing about yourself

1 Read Jodi's answers to the questions below. Complete the text about her with the words in the box.

What's your name?	Jodi Westrum
Where are you from?	the USA
How old are you?	38
What's your job?	nurse
What's your phone number?	501 889 48599
What are your favourite foods?	pasta, chocolate, bread
What's your favourite drink?	coffee
Who's your favourite singer?	Bob Marley

are	drink	from	nurse	~~name's~~
number	singer			

Hi. My (1) ___name's___ Jodi Westrum. I'm
(2) _____ the USA. I'm 38 and I'm a
(3) _____ . My phone (4) _____ is
501 889 48599. My favourite foods (5) _____
pasta, chocolate and bread. My favourite
(6) _____ is coffee and my favourite
(7) _____ is Bob Marley.

2 Look at the notes and text about Jodi and match *a–d* to *1–4*.

a) You use a comma (,) to [2]

b) You use a full stop (.) to [ ]

c) You use a question mark (?) to [ ]

d) You use *and* to [ ]

1 finish a question.

2 separate items in a list.

3 join two items.

4 finish a sentence.

3 Answer the questions about you.

What's your name?	
Where are you from?	
How old are you?	
What's your job?	
What's your phone number?	
What are your favourite foods?	
What's your favourite drink?	
Who's your favourite singer?	

4 Write about yourself. Use the answers you wrote in Exercise 3. Remember to use commas, full stops and *and*.

_____

_____

_____

_____

_____

_____

_____

Pronunciation

1 Count the number of syllables in each word. Write the number in the box.

a) twenty [2]

b) cat [ ]

c) writer [ ]

d) drink [ ]

e) singer [ ]

f) hairdresser [ ]

g) eleven [ ]

h) food [ ]

i) nurse [ ]

j) animal [ ]

🌐 07 Listen and check. Repeat the words.

2 Listen again and <u>underline</u> the stressed syllables in Exercise 1.

Example **twen**ty

3 Family

Grammar

1 Underline the correct word.

a) My **fathers'** / **father's** name is John.

b) His **sisters** / **sister's** children are twins.

c) Our **brothers** / **brother's** live in Paris.

d) Their **childrens'** / **children's** names are Max and Sam.

2 Rewrite the sentences with apostrophes (').

a) Our fathers name is John.
Our father's name is John.

b) My sisters children are two and five.

c) My mothers name is Jane.

d) My brothers names are Kelvin and Stan.

e) Paulas husbands name is Jerry.

f) Their childrens names are Ben and Stevie.

3 Write the *he* / *she* / *it* form of the verbs.

a) go   *goes*   e) watch _____

b) do   _____   f) live   _____

c) have _____   g) work   _____

d) be   _____   h) buy   _____

4 Write sentences in the present simple.

a) Sylvie / buy / food at the weekend.
Sylvie buys food at the weekend.

b) Johan / have / a big car.

c) You / like / computer games.

d) I / live / in Madrid.

e) The cat / live / in my apartment.

f) They / play / football in the park.

g) My sister / go / to bed late on Fridays.

h) I / do / the housework in our house.

i) We / eat / our meals in the kitchen.

j) He / watch / TV in the evening.

5 Write four true sentences with the verbs in Exercise 4.

Example
I play tennis with my sister.

_____

_____

_____

_____

6 Complete the text using the verbs in the box in the present simple.

~~be~~
be
buy
do
go
have
live
live
play
work

Hi. My name (1) *'s*_____ Joan. I'm from Bristol, in England. I'm an actor. This (2) _____ my family. My husband's name is Dave. He's a doctor. He (3) _____ in a hospital. He's a great husband. He (4) _____ the housework and he (5) _____ me flowers! We (6) _____ golf together at the weekend. We (7) _____ three children – a son, Mark, and two daughters, Emma and Rose. Emma (8) _____ and works in Spain. She's a waitress. Rose (9) _____ to university in Oxford. Mark (10) _____ at home with us.

🔊 08 Listen and check.

Vocabulary

1 Find the female (♀) family words in the wordsnake. Write them in the table. Which word is the same for male (♂) and female (♀)?

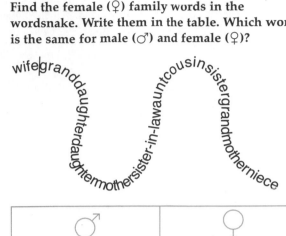

wifegranddaughterdaughtermothersister-in-lawauntcousinsistergrandmotherniece

♂	♀
husband	*wife*
brother	
son	
grandson	
father	
uncle	
cousin	
nephew	
brother-in-law	
grandfather	

2 Look at the family tree. Complete the sentences with words from Exercise 1.

Dan — Flo

Bert — John — Liz

Andy — Tracy

a) Liz is John's _____ *wife* _____ .

b) John is Liz's _____ .

c) Tracy is Andy's _____ .

d) Andy is Liz's _____ .

e) Bert is Tracy's _____ .

f) Flo is Andy's _____ .

g) Tracy is Dan's _____ .

h) Liz is Tracy's _____ .

i) Tracy is Bert's _____ .

j) Andy is Bert's _____ .

3 Write five sentences about your family using the words in Exercise 1.

Example

    Juan Carlos is Maria's son.

a) _____

b) _____

c) _____

d) _____

e) _____

4 Complete the useful phrases with the words in the box.

Call	care	Drive	forget
~~Smile!~~	time	worry	

1. Smile!
2. _____ carefully!
3. Don't _____, dear.
4. Have a good _____.
5. Take _____.
6. _____ us.
7. Don't *forget* your keys.

Listening

Monaco's Royal Family 1976

1 🔘 09 **Cover the listening script. Listen to the conversation. Write a + between a brother or sister and a − between cousins.**

Monaco's Young Royals

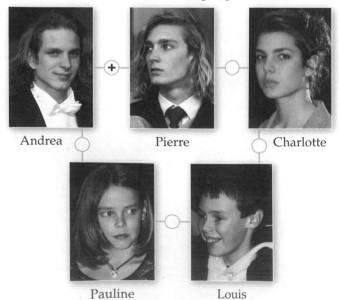

Andrea   Pierre   Charlotte

Pauline   Louis

Liam:	Who are the people in those pictures?
Anne:	They're Monaco's royal family. This one is Princess Grace and her husband, Prince Rainier, with their children – Caroline, Albert and Stephanie.
Liam:	Who's this?
Anne:	That's Andrea. He's Princess Caroline's son. So he's Rainier and Grace's grandson. And this picture is Andrea's brother, Pierre. Andrea really likes sport, especially football, but Pierre likes music. He plays the saxophone.
Liam:	Oh? And who's this?
Anne:	That's their sister, Charlotte. She likes sport, too. Especially horse-riding and skiing.
Liam:	Is Prince Albert her uncle?
Anne:	Prince Albert is Caroline's brother, so yes, he's Charlotte's uncle.
Liam:	And the girl in this photo? Is she another sister?
Anne:	No, that's Pauline. She's Stephanie's daughter. And that's Pauline's brother, Louis.
Liam:	So they're Andrea, Pierre and Charlotte's cousins?
Anne:	Yes. And they're all Rainier and Grace's grandchildren.
Liam:	I see.

2 **Listen again and <u>underline</u> the correct answer.**

a) Andrea is **<u>Caroline's</u> / Stephanie's** son.

b) Pierre is Andrea's **son / brother**.

c) Pierre's sister is **Pauline / Charlotte**.

d) Charlotte likes **football / skiing**.

e) Prince **Albert / Rainier** is Caroline's brother.

f) Louis's mother is **Caroline / Stephanie**.

g) Pauline is Charlotte's **daughter / cousin**.

3 **Are the statements true (T) or false (F)?**

a) Caroline and Stephanie are sisters. __*T*__

b) Andrea plays the saxophone. _____

c) Albert is Charlotte's uncle. _____

d) Pauline is Stephanie's daughter. _____

e) Pauline and Louis are cousins. _____

f) Pierre is Prince Rainier's grandson. _____

Writing

1 Read the text and then tick (✓) the correct rules.

Andrea, Charlotte and Pierre are Princess Caroline's children. Their cousins, Pauline and Louis, are Princess Stephanie's children. Their uncle is Prince Albert. He's the son of Prince Rainier and Princess Grace of Monaco.

You use an apostrophe

a) in contractions ('*m*, '*s* etc.) ☐

b) with plural *s* ☐

c) to write about possession ☐

2 Rewrite the text about Michael Douglas with apostrophes.

Michaels childrens names are Dylan and Carys. Michaels American. Hes married to Catherine. Shes from Wales. Her parents names are Dai and Pat, and Michaels parents names are Kirk and Diana. Dylan and Carys have cousins in Britain and America.

_____

_____

_____

_____

_____

_____

3 Draw a family tree and write about a family you know.

_____

_____

_____

_____

_____

_____

_____

_____

Pronunciation

1 🔘 10 Listen and repeat the words in the box.

~~brother~~	buy	drink	eight	game
know	late	make	~~mother~~	Mr	name
play	sister	so	stay	steak	think	try

2 Put the words in the box into pairs of rhyming words.

a) ___*brother*___ and ___*mother*___

b) _____ and _____

c) _____ and _____

d) _____ and _____

e) _____ and _____

f) _____ and _____

g) _____ and _____

h) _____ and _____

i) _____ and _____

🔘 11 Listen and check.

4 Different

Grammar

1 Write sentences in the present simple.

a) My sister / have / two children.
My sister has two children.

b) I / like / football.
_____

c) My father / work / in a bank.
_____

d) My friends / play / football every weekend.
_____

e) My aunt / live / in Tokyo.
_____

f) We / go / on holiday every year.
_____

2 Write questions.

a) you / speak Spanish?
Do you speak Spanish?

b) your father / drink beer?
_____

c) you / like hip-hop?
_____

d) your mother / play tennis?
_____

e) you / do the housework?
_____

f) your friend / sing in a band?
_____

3 Write true short answers to the questions in Exercise 2.

Example
Yes, I do. / No, I don't.

a) _____
b) _____
c) _____
d) _____
e) _____
f) _____

4 Complete the sentences with the negative of the verb in bold.

a) I **speak** German but I ___*don't speak*___ Italian.

b) She **likes** swimming but she _____ football.

c) He **plays** the guitar but he _____ the piano.

d) They **work** in a restaurant but they _____ _____ at the weekend.

e) He **sings** in a band but he _____ in the shower.

f) She **drinks** tea but she _____ beer.

5 Complete the text with the words in the box.

| her | him | it | ~~me~~ | them | us | you |

Send Chat Attach Address Fonts Colors Save As Draft

Dear Eva

This is a picture of (1) __*me*__ and my boyfriend. His name's Tom. My parents don't like (2) _____ but I think he's great. My parents don't like my friends, so I don't listen to (3) _____ .

My sister likes Tom and he likes (4) _____ , so that's good. Every weekend Tom and I watch football, and my sister comes with (5) _____ .

What about (6) _____ ? How's your new job? Do you like (7) _____ ?

Love

Michelle

Vocabulary

1 Label the activities with the verbs in the box.

cooking	dancing	driving	jogging
reading	shopping	studying	~~swimming~~

a)   _swimming_

b)   _____

c)   _____

d)   _____

e)   _____

f)   _____

g)   _____

h)   _____

2 Match a face with a feeling.

a) ☺   I don't like it.

b) ☹   I like it.

c) 👍☺   I don't mind it.

d) ☺   I really like it.

e) ♥☺   I hate it.

f) ☹👎   I love it.

3 Use the pictures and write sentences.

a) I ♥☺

I love swimming. _____

b) I ☹

_____

c) I ☹👎

_____

d) I ☺

_____

e) I 👍☺

_____

f) I ☺

_____

4 Tick (✓) the statements in Exercise 3 which are true for you.

5 Complete the conversation with *what*, *think* or *about*.

Calum: (1) __What__ do you (2) _____ of the new James Bond?

Suzy: I (3) _____ he's awful. What (4) _____ you?

Calum: I (5) _____ he's great.

Suzy: Mm. And (6) _____ do you (7) _____ of Beyoncé's new album?

Calum: I don't know. (8) _____ (9) _____ you?

Suzy: I (10) _____ it's boring.

Calum: Mm, yes, I prefer Mary J. Blige.

🌐 12 Listen and check.

Different   UNIT 4   **17**

Reading

1   Read the emails from Marek and Shawna.
    Tick (✓) the true sentence.

    a)   They work together.   ☐

    b)   They are brother and sister.   ☐

    c)   They are new email friends.   ☐

2   Read the emails again. Are these statements
    true (T) or false (F)?

    a)   Marek is a student.   _T_

    b)   Marek's family doesn't live in a house.   _____

    c)   Marek thinks Razorlight are boring.   _____

    d)   Shawna lives with her sister.   _____

    e)   Shawna likes her job.   _____

    f)   Shawna stays at home at weekends.   _____

3   Cover the emails. What do you remember about
    Marek and Shawna? Answer the questions.

    a)   How old is Marek?

    _____

    b)   Does Marek live with his grandparents?

    _____

    c)   What are Marek's favourite sports?

    _____

    d)   Does Shawna like dancing?

    _____

    e)   Does Shawna like sport?

    _____

    f)   What does Shawna do every weekend?

    _____

Send   Chat   Attach   Address   Fonts   Colors   Save As Draft

Hi Shawna

My name is Marek. I'm from Gdansk in Poland. I'm 18
and I'm a student at Gdansk University. Are you at
university?

I live with my parents and two sisters in a small apartment
in the city. What about you? Do you live at home?

I like all kinds of sport, but my favourite sports are football
and swimming. Do you like sport?

I really love music. Razorlight is my favourite band. What
music do you like?

Write soon.
Your friend,
Marek :–)

Send   Chat   Attach   Address   Fonts   Colors   Save As Draft

Hi Marek

Thanks for your email. I live in Boston in the USA. I'm 20.
No, I'm not at university – I work in a shop called Gap. Do
you know it? I love clothes, so it's a good job for me! :–)

I don't live at home. I live in an apartment with my best
friend, Selma.

I don't really like sport – and I hate football! It's boring.

I love music and dancing. I have lots of friends and I go out
every weekend. I like rap music. Do you like the Beastie
Boys? They're great!

Write soon.
Shawna :–)

Writing

1 Match the beginnings (*a–e*) of the punctuation rules with the endings (*1–5*).

a) You use a full stop ☐ 4

b) You use a question mark ☐

c) You use a capital letter ☐

d) You use a comma ☐

e) You use an apostrophe ☐

1 at the end of a question.
2 to separate items in a list.
3 for contractions and for possession.
4 at the end of a sentence.
5 to start a sentence and when you write names.

2 Write the email with the correct punctuation.

> Send Chat Attach Address Fonts Colors Save As Draft
>
> hi
>
> my names john im 32 and im from england i live in leeds and im a sales manager i have three brothers and two sisters my mums a doctor and my dads a bus driver
>
> what about you do you have a large family
>
> i like swimming jogging and sailing my favourite activity is cooking i really love it i work in my brothers restaurant at the weekends
>
> do you like sport do you like cooking
>
> write and tell me about yourself
>
> your friend john

3 Write an email to a new e-friend.

● Write sentences about yourself and your family.

● Say what you like and don't like.

● Ask your new friend questions about his/her life.

Remember to check your punctuation.

> Send Chat Attach Address Fonts Colors Save As Draft

Pronunciation

1 🔘 13 Listen to the sounds /æ/ and /ɑː/.

/æ/ animal

/ɑː/ apartment

2 🔘 14 Listen to the words in the box. Is the **underlined** sound /æ/ or /ɑː/? Put the words in the correct column.

> ~~animal~~ ~~apartment~~ aunt band car
> chat dancing family father handbag
> have large man partner

/æ/	/ɑː/
animal	apartment

🔘 15 Listen again and check.

5 Days

Grammar

1 Complete the texts with the verbs in the boxes.

do   get up   have

Jemma (1) _gets up_ at seven thirty. She
(2) _____ exercise in the gym before work.
She (3) _____ breakfast at work.

have   read   work

Louis (4) _____ in the city. He (5) _____
lunch at one o'clock. He (6) _____ the
newspaper every day.

go   have   watch

Pat and Lyle (7) _____ dinner at eight o'clock.
Later, they (8) _____ television. They
(9) _____ to bed at midnight.

2 Write the time in two different ways.

a) _It's eleven fifteen._
It's quarter past eleven.

b) _____
_____

c) _____
_____

d) _____
_____

e) _____
_____

f) _____
_____

g) _____
_____

h) _____
_____

3 Write questions with *What time?*

a) you / get up
What time do you get up?

b) you / have breakfast
_____

c) you / go to work
_____

d) you / have dinner
_____

e) you / go to bed
_____

4 Write true answers to the questions in Exercise 3.
Example (a)
I get up at six thirty.

a) _____
b) _____
c) _____
d) _____
e) _____

Vocabulary

1 Complete the days of the week.

Monday	**F**
T	**Sa**
W	**Su**
Th	

What's your favourite day of the week?

_____

2 Complete the conversations with the words in the box.

~~How~~	Can	is	it	please	receipt	Thank

Conversation 1

Man: (1) ___How___ much is (2) _____
                  to the station?

Taxi driver: Twelve pounds.

Man: Can I have a (3) _____ , please?

Taxi driver: OK.

Man: (4) _____ you.

Conversation 2

Woman: How much (5) _____ a bottle of
               beer?

Barman: Three euros.

Woman: Two beers, (6) _____ .

Barman: (7) _____ I see your ID?

Woman: OK.

🔊 **16 Listen and check.**

3 Complete the table with the verb phrases in the box.

~~to bed~~   ~~breakfast~~   dinner   a good time
home   lunch   on the internet   out
shopping   a shower   to work

have	go
breakfast	_to bed_
_____	_____
_____	_____
_____	_____
_____	_____

4 Look at the pictures and complete the text about Connie's day with the verbs in Exercise 3.

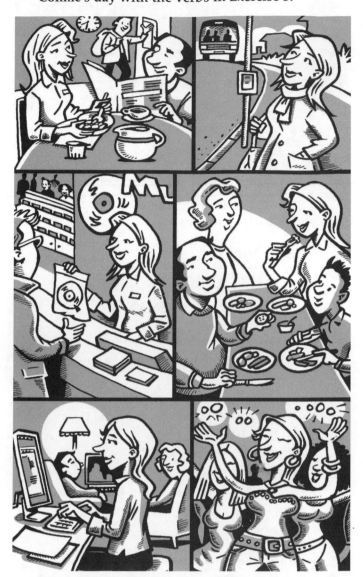

On weekdays I get up at about eight o'clock. First I
(1) ___have a shower___ . Then I (2) _____
_____ – a cup of tea, a banana, cereal and
toast. At about nine o'clock I leave the house and
(3) _____ . I work in a music shop in
London. I love it! The shop opens at ten. I work
all morning and then I (4) _____ at
half past one – sandwiches in a café. The shop
closes at five o'clock, and I (5) _____ .
In the evening I (6) _____ with my
family at home and then watch TV or use the
computer. I like to (7) _____ or
email my friends. I (8) _____ at
midnight.
It's different at the weekend! On Saturday afternoon
I (9) _____ . I buy CDs and clothes.
On Saturday night I (10) _____ with
my friends. I love dancing. We always
(11) _____ .

🔊 **17 Listen and check.**

Listening

1 🔘 **18–19 Cover the listening script. Listen and complete the sentences with the names in the box.**

> Toby   Alana

a) _____ stays in the city centre all day.

b) _____ goes to the beach.

2 **Listen again and <u>underline</u> the correct answer.**

a) Toby's favourite restaurant is <u>La Cucina</u> / **Bondi**.

b) The beach is **in** / **near** Sydney.

c) Toby's perfect evening is to spend time with his **family** / **friends**.

d) Alana likes **sushi** / **eggs** for breakfast.

e) Alana goes shopping with her **sister** / **friend**.

f) Alana's boyfriend is called **Michel** / **Luc**.

g) After dinner Alana goes **dancing** / **to the cinema**.

3 **Complete the notes. Listen again and check.**

TOBY *My perfect day*

> BREAKFAST (1) _*coffee*_ and sandwich, in a café
> MORNING go to (2) _____ , buy
> (3) _____
> HAVE LUNCH IN (4) _____ restaurant
> AFTERNOON go to the (5) _____ with
> (6) _____
> EVENING eat, (7) _____ and talk to my friends

ALANA *My perfect day*

> MORNING go to Vancouver city centre, go
> (8) _____ with (9) _____
> HAVE LUNCH IN (10) _____ restaurant
> AFTERNOON go to the (11) _____ with
> (12) _____
> EVENING have dinner at a (13) _____
> restaurant with my boyfriend

Interviewer: Toby, tell us about your perfect day.

Toby: Well, I have a coffee and a sandwich in a café near my house and then I go to the city centre – Sydney city centre – and buy clothes.

Interviewer: With a friend?

Toby: No, alone. I don't like shopping with other people. I have lunch at La Cucina, my favourite Italian restaurant. Pasta, of course. And then, in the afternoon, I go to the beach with my friends.

Interviewer: Is there a beach in Sydney?

Toby: Oh, yes! My favourite is Bondi. It's beautiful. After that, in the evening, my friends come to my house and we eat salad, listen to music and talk. Perfect!

Interviewer: Thanks, Toby.

Interviewer: Alana, tell us about your perfect day.

Alana: Yes, OK. In the morning I have eggs for breakfast. Then I get ready and go to Vancouver city centre. I go shopping in the morning with my friend Makiko.

Interviewer: And what about lunch?

Alana: We have sushi in my favourite Japanese restaurant. It's called Sakura. In the afternoon I go to the cinema with my sister and watch a film.

Interviewer: And in the evening?

Alana: I have dinner at a French restaurant called Michel with my boyfriend, Luc. After dinner we go dancing and then go home.

Interviewer: Thanks, Alana.

Pronunciation

1 🔘 **20 Listen and <u>underline</u> the words B stresses.**

1 **A:** Your name is Simon Jones.
  B: No, my name is Simon <u>Johns</u>.

2 **A:** You live in New Orleans.
  B: No, I live in New York.

2 **Contradict each statement. Use the words (in brackets) and stress the different information.**

a) You have two brothers and two sisters. (one sister) *No, I have two brothers and <u>one</u> sister.*

b) You like swimming and cycling. (swimming and tennis)

c) You're a lorry driver. (taxi driver)

d) Your brother's a lawyer. (mother)

e) You have lunch at home. (dinner)

f) You love eating in French restaurants. (Italian)

🔘 **21 Listen and check.**

Writing

Sequencing: *then*, *after* (*that*)
Describing a perfect day

1 **Complete the summary of Alana's perfect day with *After* or *Then*.**

She goes shopping in the morning. (1) ___*Then*___ she has lunch at her favourite restaurant. (2) _____ lunch she goes to the cinema. She has dinner with her boyfriend. (3) _____ that, they go dancing. (4) _____ they go home.

🔘 **22 Listen and check.**

2 **Complete the rules with *After* and *Then*.**

a) _____ is used to introduce the next thing that happens.

b) _____ is also used to introduce the next thing that happens, but it is followed by a noun (*breakfast, lunch, dinner, that,* etc.).

3 **Use the notes about Zana's perfect day and complete the text.**

	Name:	Zana
Morning:	**What:**	go shopping
	Where:	(Prague) city centre
	Who with:	Tomas
Afternoon:	**What:**	museum
	Where:	the National Gallery
	Who with:	Tomas
Evening:	**What:**	Swan Lake (ballet)
	Where:	the National Theatre
	Who with:	Tomas

A perfect day

I meet Tomas at 10.00 a.m. and we drive to
(1) ___*Prague*___ . In the morning we go
(2) _____ . Then we have lunch at a café.
After lunch, in the afternoon, we go to the National
Gallery – it's a beautiful (3) _____ . We have
an early dinner at the Bellevue. After that we go to
the (4) _____ _____ and watch
(5) _____ _____ , my favourite
(6) _____ . We drive home at midnight, at
the end of a perfect day.

4 **Think about how to spend your perfect day. Complete the notes.**

Morning: What? _____
Where? _____
Who with? _____

Afternoon: What? _____
Where? _____
Who with? _____

Evening: What? _____
Where? _____
Who with? _____

5 **Write about your perfect day. Use your notes in Exercise 4 to help you. Use *then* and *after* (+ noun).**

6 Living

Grammar

1 Write the words in the correct order.

a) loud   to   music   I   listen   .
I listen to loud music.

b) in   city   the   I   live   .

_____

c) drive   a   My   Porsche   parents   .

_____

d) homework   teacher   gives   Our   us   .

_____

e) do   housework   the   I   .

_____

f) tea   a lot of   My   drinks   father   .

_____

g) breakfast   family   together   has   My   .

_____

2 Write the negative of each sentence in Exercise 1.

a) *I don't listen to loud music.*
b) _____
c) _____
d) _____
e) _____
f) _____
g) _____

3 Tick (✓) the sentences in Exercises 1 and 2 that are true for you.

4 Add the adverbs to the sentences.

a) Fiona goes to Italy for her holidays. (sometimes)
Fiona sometimes goes to Italy for her holidays.

b) Ali's late for class. (hardly ever)

_____

c) I train at the weekend. (always)

_____

d) They're open on Sunday. (never)

_____

e) Do you go to bed after midnight? (ever)

_____

f) She's at work until 7.30 p.m. (usually)

_____

5 Put the words in the box in the correct column.

| 15th May   January   night   seven o'clock |
| Sunday   the evening   the spring |
| the weekend   Tuesday morning |

on	in	at
15th May	_____	_____
_____	_____	_____
_____	_____	_____

6 Complete the text with *on*, *in* or *at*.

I love exercise. I usually get up (1) _at_ 6.30 (2) ____ the morning. (3) ____ Monday and Tuesday I go swimming. (4) ____ the winter I go to the gym (5) ____ night and (6) ____ the summer I go jogging (7) ____ the evening. (8) ____ Wednesday and Thursday morning I go for a long walk with my dog. (9) ____ the weekend I play football.

🔊 23 Listen and check.

Vocabulary

1 Find twelve months of the year and write them in the table below. Look → and ↓ .

Q	F	U	D	J	U	I	L	O	M	B	N
U	S	E	P	T	E	M	B	E	R	N	O
D	T	Y	U	M	D	K	K	A	I	B	V
X	K	P	R	M	S	L	W	C	N	R	E
H	K	L	I	J	U	L	Y	X	M	S	M
J	A	J	T	U	M	E	Y	S	U	I	B
A	R	U	M	A	U	R	B	A	E	L	E
N	V	N	F	A	U	G	U	S	T	N	R
U	D	E	S	W	N	P	S	H	L	I	P
A	D	R	A	G	M	A	Y	S	L	A	F
R	W	H	E	R	E	X	A	N	B	C	E
Y	G	I	M	A	R	C	H	R	A	H	B
A	R	N	O	P	U	I	N	D	A	B	R
B	O	C	T	O	B	E	R	U	P	H	U
S	E	T	T	E	T	S	E	J	R	I	A
D	E	C	E	M	B	E	R	U	I	U	R
A	G	T	U	P	L	S	W	Q	L	J	Y

Spring	Summer	Autumn	Winter
_____	_____	_____	_____
_____	_____	_____	_____
_____	_____	_____	_____
_____	_____	_____	_____

2 <u>Underline</u> the correct word.

a) My mother **does** / **makes** my washing for me.

b) I usually **do** / **make** my homework from 7.00 p.m. to 8.00 p.m.

c) I **do** / **make** a lot of phone calls every day.

d) I **do** / **make** the shopping once a week.

e) My father never **does** / **makes** the washing up.

f) I love cooking – I like **doing** / **making** dinner for my friends.

g) I hate **doing** / **making** the housework.

h) I don't usually **do** / **make** a lot of noise. I never listen to loud music.

3 Tick (✓) the sentences in Exercise 1 that are true for you.

Change three sentences that you didn't tick to make them true for you.

Example (a)

My mother doesn't do my washing for me. _____

_____

_____

4 Give the dates in two ways.

a) 02/02
We write _2nd February_
We say _the second of February_

b) 15/03
We write _____
We say _____

c) 01/06
We write _____
We say _____

d) 28/11
We write _____
We say _____

e) 31/12
We write _____
We say _____

5 Complete the conversation with the words in the box.

closed	closes	~~don't~~
open	opens	time

Cathy: John, we (1) _don't_ have any coffee for breakfast. Can you go and get some? Please!

John: It's midnight. The shops are (2) _____ .

Cathy: No, the supermarket (3) _____ at one o'clock.

John Hm. What (4) _____ does it (5) _____ ?

Cathy: It (6) _____ at half past six. Why?

John: You can go in the morning. Now go to sleep.

🌐 24 **Listen and check.**

Listening

1 🔘 25 **Cover the listening script. Listen to Eleanor talking about the festival Halloween. Circle the words you hear.**

fun	school	costumes	beer
parade	party	dancing	food
music	sweets	fireworks	

2 **Listen again. Are the sentences true (T) or false (F)?**

a) Eleanor thinks Halloween is great. _T_

b) Halloween is on 1st October. _____

c) The teachers don't wear costumes. _____

d) Last year Eleanor was a rabbit. _____

e) The children have lessons in the morning.
    _____

f) Children don't do homework at Halloween.
    _____

g) The children go to bed at six o'clock. _____

3 **Answer the questions.**

a) Does Eleanor like Halloween?
    Yes, she does.

b) What do parents do at school at Halloween?
    _____

c) What do the children do at the school party?
    _____

d) Where do Eleanor and her family go in the evening?
    _____

e) What do Eleanor's parents wear in the evening?
    _____

f) What do people give the children?
    _____

Evie:	Tell me about Halloween, Eleanor.
Eleanor:	Halloween is really great. A lot of fun.
Evie:	When is it?
Eleanor:	It's on the last day of October, the 31st. All the children at my school wear costumes. All the teachers too! Last year I was a cat, and my sister was a rabbit.
Evie:	What happens at school? Do you have lessons?
Eleanor:	Yes, we have normal lessons in the morning, but at lunchtime there's a parade and all the students walk around the school. All the parents come to school to watch the parade. In the afternoon there aren't any lessons. Every class has a party.
Evie:	What happens at the party?
Eleanor:	We play games and eat special Halloween food.
Evie:	And what do you do after school?
Eleanor:	We go home on the bus, do our homework and have dinner. Then at about six o'clock in the evening we go to a street party in Perry Avenue, a street near my house.
Evie:	Do you wear your costumes to the party?
Eleanor:	Yes. Everybody wears funny costumes – even my mum and dad! And all my friends are there. We go to all the houses in the street and people give us sweets. My sister and I always go to bed really late at Halloween!

Pronunciation

1 🔘 26 **Listen to the ways of pronouncing the final _s_ in the third person present simple.**

/z/ drive_s_   /s/ drink_s_   /ɪz/ finish_es_

2 🔘 27 **Listen to the verbs in the box. Is the underlined sound /z/ or /s/ or /ɪz/? Put the verbs in the correct column.**

~~drink_s_~~	~~drive_s_~~	~~finish_es_~~	goe_s_	ha_s_
like_s_	listen_s_	live_s_	start_s_	take_s_
teach_es_	visit_s_	watch_es_		

/z/	/s/	/ɪz/
drives	_drinks_	_finishes_
_____	_____	_____
_____	_____	_____
_____	_____	
_____	_____	

🔘 28 **Listen and check. Repeat the verbs.**

Writing

1 Read a description of a festival. Match the
paragraphs (*1–4*) with what they describe (*a–d*).

a) What people do/eat/drink at the festival _ 4 _

b) What happens at the festival _____

c) The date of the festival and how long it lasts

_____

d) The name of the festival and where it takes
place _____

Bonfire Night

1 Bonfire Night takes place in Britain.

2 It's on 5th November and goes on for one night.

3 There is a bonfire and there are fireworks. In
my town, Lewes, there is also a big parade in
the town and people wear colourful costumes.

4 People stand around the bonfire and watch the
fireworks. They drink wine or beer and eat
sausages.

2 Think of a festival you know. Write notes about
the festival.

a) The name of the festival and where it takes
place

_____

b) The date of the festival and how long it lasts

_____

c) What happens at the festival

_____

_____

d) What people eat/drink/do at the festival

_____

_____

3 Complete the sentences to describe the festival in
Exercise 2.

> **1** _____ (name of festival)
> takes place in _____
> (name of town/country where the festival
> takes place).
>
> **2** It starts on / It's on _____
> (day) and goes on for
> _____ (how long).
>
> **3** There is/are _____ and
> _____ (what happens at
> the festival) .
>
> **4** People _____ and
> _____ (what people do/
> eat/drink at the festival).

4 Write a description of your festival. Use the
sentences you completed in Exercise 3 and the
description in Exercise 1 to help you.

7 Sea

Grammar

1 Write the past forms of the regular verbs.

a) ask   _asked_   f) work _____
b) phone _____   g) study _____
c) love _____   h) watch _____
d) want _____   i) start _____
e) play _____   j) stop _____

2 Choose a verb from Exercise 1 to complete each sentence.

a) Yesterday I _studied_ these regular verbs.

b) We _____ a great film on TV last night.

c) Carole _____ you when you were out.

d) You're late. The film _____ ten minutes ago.

e) Brad always _____ to be an actor.

f) You _____ a good game of tennis last week.

3 Complete the table.

Irregular verbs	
Present simple	**Past simple**
be	_was / were_
break	_____
_____	came
do	_____
_____	had
say	_____
_____	saw
_____	sold
sit	_____
take	_____

4 Write questions with *When was the last time you ...?*

a) go / to the cinema?

When was the last time you went to the cinema?

b) read / a good book?

_____

c) wear / blue?

_____

d) lose / something?

_____

5 Write true answers to the questions in Exercise 4.

Example (a)

Last Friday. I saw Mission Impossible III.

a) _____

b) _____

c) _____

d) _____

6 Complete the text using the past simple form of the verbs.

Thor Heyerdahl (1) _was_ (be) born in Larvik, Norway in 1914. He (2) _____ (study) geography and anthropology. He (3) _____ (want) to find out if people in the past (4) _____ (can) travel long distances by boat. In 1947 he (5) _____ (make) a simple boat – a raft – called Kon Tiki and (6) _____ (sail) 8,000 kilometres from South America to the Tuamotu Islands in the Pacific Ocean. On the boat they (7) _____ (have) nothing but a radio, some food and fresh water. People all over the world (8) _____ (watch) and (9) _____ (listen) to the story of Kon Tiki's journey. In 2006 Thor's grandson Olav Heyerdahl and five other men (10) _____ (make) the same journey as his grandfather. They (11) _____ (see) fish, birds and sharks. The journey (12) _____ (take) 93 days.

🌐 29 Listen and check.

Vocabulary

1 Find the words for seven water sports in the wordsquare and label the pictures below. Look → and ↓ .

W	I	N	D	S	U	R	F	I	N	G
I	S	W	I	W	B	A	G	H	E	E
L	A	D	F	I	S	H	I	N	G	S
E	I	S	T	M	U	D	V	W	N	U
O	L	N	T	M	E	S	E	O	L	R
K	I	E	O	I	T	H	I	H	I	F
A	N	D	E	N	A	I	A	H	M	I
H	G	I	N	G	S	P	B	S	R	N
K	I	T	E	S	U	R	F	I	N	G
L	D	E	I	A	N	E	S	A	I	W
S	C	U	B	A	D	I	V	I	N	G

a) _windsurfing_

e) _____

b) _____

f) _____

c) _____

g) _____

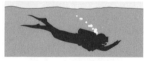

d) _____

2 Today is Monday 10th July, 2000. Use time expressions to describe these dates.

a) Friday 7th July, 2000

   last Friday / three days ago

b) Monday 3rd July, 2000

c) 10th July, 1999

d) 10th January, 2000

e) Sunday 9th July, 2000

3 Complete the story with the time linkers in the box.

> After   At first   eventually   later
> ~~One day~~   Suddenly

Ten years ago I went on holiday to a house in the country with some friends. (1) _One day_ we decided to go for a walk near the house.

(2) _____ it was sunny. We walked and chatted. It was perfect. (3) _____ two hours we came to a beach, but we didn't know where we were. We decided to go back to the house.

(4) _____ it got very cold and it started to snow. We walked and we walked. Three hours (5) _____ we found a road.

We walked along the road and (6) _____ we came to a pub. It was seven o'clock at night and we were 20 miles from our house. That night we stayed in the pub. Someone drove us home in the morning.

🔘 **30 Listen and check.**

4 Write sentences about the weather in these cities.

London		Madrid
Paris		Bangkok
Rio de Janeiro		New York

In London it's foggy.

_____

_____

_____

_____

What's the weather like in your city today?

_____

Reading

1 🌐 **31 Read the story. Tick (✓) the picture described in the story.**

a

b

2 Read the story again and underline the correct answer.

a) Paul lived in **India** / **Yemen**.

b) One day he went **swimming** / **to the beach** with his mother.

c) When Paul went into the sea, his mother started **reading** / **listening to the radio**.

d) At first, Paul **stayed near** / **was a long way from** the beach.

e) Paul saw two **dolphins** / **sharks** in the water.

f) The man in the boat took Paul to **hospital** / **the beach**.

3 Read the story again and answer the questions.

a) What did Paul and his family often do?

They often went swimming in the Indian Ocean.

b) What was the weather like on the day of the story?

_____

c) What did Paul and his mother do after half an hour?

_____

d) Who spoke to Paul?

_____

e) How did Paul feel when he looked in the water?

_____

f) What did Paul do when he returned three weeks later?

_____

One sunny day

When he was ten, Paul lived in Yemen. Paul and his family often went swimming in the Indian Ocean.

One day, Paul went to the beach with his mother. It was a hot, sunny day and Paul went into the sea on his airbed. His mother started reading a book.

After about half an hour, Paul went to sleep on his airbed on the water and his mother went to sleep on the beach. At first, Paul stayed near the beach, but then the sea started pushing him away from the beach.

Suddenly, Paul woke up. He was a long way from the beach. He heard a man's voice. 'Don't move,' said the man. Paul didn't move. The boat came near and the man took Paul into the boat. Paul looked into the sea and saw two enormous sharks. He was terrified.

Eventually, the boat returned to the beach. Paul found his mother and told her about his experience.

Three weeks later, Paul and his mother returned to the same place, but this time Paul decided to stay with his mother on the beach.

Pronunciation

1 🌐 **32 Listen to the three different ways of pronouncing the ending of regular verbs in the past simple.**

/d/ call**ed**

/t/ ask**ed**

/ɪd/ need**ed**

2 🌐 **33 Listen to the verbs in the box. Is the underlined sound /d/ or /t/ or /ɪd/? Put the verbs in the correct column.**

~~ask**ed**~~   ~~call**ed**~~   finish**ed**   lik**ed**   listen**ed** liv**ed**   lov**ed**   ~~need**ed**~~   play**ed**   repeat**ed** shout**ed**   start**ed**   stopp**ed**   talk**ed**   us**ed** wait**ed**   want**ed**   watch**ed**

/d/	/t/	/ɪd/
called	*asked*	*needed*
_____	_____	_____
_____	_____	_____
_____	_____	_____
_____	_____	_____
_____	_____	_____

🌐 **34 Listen and check. Repeat the verbs.**

Writing

Using time expressions
Telling a story

1 Look at the story on page 30. Match the stages of writing a story (*1–4*) with the time expressions (*a–d*) below.

1 Introduce the time, place and characters _*c*_

2 Start the story _____

3 Continue the story _____

4 End the story _____

a Two days later
Eventually

b At first
Suddenly
After half an hour

c A few years ago
A long time ago
In 2006
When he was ten

d One day

2 Put this story in the correct order. Think about the time expressions.

At first, they did well and enjoyed themselves. ☐

Suddenly, the wind took Sebastian and his windsurfing board out to sea. Sebastian was terrified and Eve was very worried. ☐

Five minutes later, a boat went out to find Sebastian. ☐

In 2006, Eve and Sebastian Rankin went to Sicily on holiday. *1*

Eventually the boat returned, with Sebastian. ☐

After an hour, the weather got cold and windy. ☐

One day, Eve and Sebastian decided to go windsurfing for the first time. ☐

3 Write a short story about something that happened to you when you were young. Use some of the time expressions in Exercise 1.

8 Alone

Grammar

1 Write sentences in the past simple.

a) I / like / spiders.
   I liked spiders.

b) I / go / to school.
   _____

c) I / live / in a different city.
   _____

d) I / work / at the weekend.
   _____

e) I / listen / to rock music.
   _____

f) I / enjoy / my life.
   _____

2 Write questions for the sentences in Exercise 1.
   a) *Did you like spiders?*
   b) _____
   c) _____
   d) _____
   e) _____
   f) _____

3 Write true answers to the questions in Exercise 2 about your life five years ago.

   Example (a)

   No, I didn't. But I don't mind them now.
   a) _____
   b) _____
   c) _____
   d) _____
   e) _____
   f) _____

4 Complete the text with the verbs (in brackets) in the past simple.

Howard Hughes
(1) ____was____ (be) born in 1905 in Texas, USA.
He (2) _____ (lose) both of his parents before he was twenty. They (3) _____ (leave) him a lot of money.

In 1925, he (4) _____ (get) married. He and his wife (5) _____ (move) to Hollywood and he (6) _____ (start) work as a film director. In 1929, he and his wife got divorced. He (7) _____ (have) love affairs with a lot of Hollywood actresses.

Later in life, Hughes (8) _____ (become) more and more private. In the 1960s he (9) _____ (stop) going out in public. He (10) _____ (die) in 1976. At the end of his life he had a lot of money, but no friends.

🔘 **35 Listen and check.**

5 Complete the questions for each answer.

a) What *was Freddie Mercury's real name?*
   His real name was Farrokh Bulsara.

b) When _____
   He was born in 1946, in Zanzibar.

c) Where _____
   He grew up in India.

d) What _____
   He was a singer.

e) _____ any children?
   No, he didn't have any children.

f) When _____
   He died in 1991.

Vocabulary

1 Find the adjectives in the wordsnake and write them under the correct picture.

interested bored sad excited nervous angry frightened embarassed

a) _____

b) _interested_

c) _____

d) _____

e) _____

f) _____

g) _____

h) _____

2 Complete the text with *about*, *in*, *of* or *with*.

Ewa Borkowska is happy (1) _about_ crossing the Sahara Desert alone. 'I'm not worried (2) _____ getting hungry and I'm not frightened (3) _____ snakes,' she said. 'Everything is ready. The only problem is the camels. They aren't easy animals – I often get angry (4) _____ them.' But how long does she want the journey to take? 'I'm not interested (5) _____ winning any races, I'm just excited (6) _____ having the chance to do it.'

🔘 **36 Listen and check.**

3 Complete the conversations with the phrases *Let's* or *Why don't you*.

Dean: I'm tired.
Jackie: (1) _Why don't you_ go to bed?
Dean: Mmm. Good idea.

Sean: I'm hungry.
Kate: Me too. (2) _____ have lunch.
Sean: Great idea!

Emma: Mum, I'm bored.
Mother: (3) _____ go for a walk?
Emma: No, thank you. What's on TV?

André: I'm hot.
Sabine: Me too. (4) _____ go for a swim in the lake.
André: Yes, and (5) _____ take some food with us. We can have a picnic.

Julie: Excuse me. Do you know where King Street is, please?
Dave: Sorry, I'm not sure. (6) _____ ask that police officer over there?
Julie: Yes, that's a good idea. Thank you.

🔘 **37 Listen and check.**

Reading

1 🌐 38 **Read the article about Ellen MacArthur and answer the question.**

What does she do?

_____

Around the world alone

ELLEN MACARTHUR was born on 8 July 1976 in Derbyshire, England. When she was eight years old, her aunt took her sailing and Ellen fell in love with the sea. She didn't live near the sea, so she couldn't learn to sail, but Ellen spent a lot of time reading stories and books about sailing. She saved all her money and bought a boat. When she was a child, Ellen wanted to work with animals. But when she was 17, she changed her mind and decided to become a sailor.

When she was 18, Ellen sailed round Britain alone in her boat _Iduna_. Then, in 1997, when she was 20, Ellen went to France. She learned French, bought a boat called _Le Poisson_ ('the fish') and did a lot of work on it. She sailed _Le Poisson_ 3,000 miles across the Atlantic in the Mini Transat solo race and finished 17th.

In 2005, Ellen became world-famous when she sailed her boat 27,000 miles around the world alone. The journey took 71 days, 14 hours and 18 minutes and she broke the world record. Was Ellen frightened on that journey? 'Yes,' she said. But she wasn't lonely. 'I never needed anyone,' she said. 'Sailing is my job and I get to do what I love every day. It's a fantastic job and I'm very lucky.'

2 **Read the article again and number the events in order, 1–6.**

a) She bought her first boat. ☐

b) She sailed solo around the world. ☐

c) Ellen went sailing with her aunt. ☐ _1_

d) She sailed across the Atlantic. ☐

e) She read a lot of books about sailing. ☐

f) She sailed around Britain alone. ☐

3 **Are the statements true (T) or false (F)?**

a) Derbyshire is near the sea. _F_

b) Ellen's aunt bought her first boat. _____

c) When she was eight, Ellen wanted to be a doctor. _____

d) Ellen decided to become a sailor when she was 17. _____

e) Ellen bought a boat in France. _____

f) Ellen won the Mini Transat solo race when she was 17. _____

g) The round-the-world trip was 27,000 miles. _____

h) Ellen is never frightened of the sea. _____

Pronunciation

1 🌐 39 **Listen to the questions. Which speaker sounds bored and which speaker sounds interested? Write _bored_ or _interested_.**

Speaker A: Do you like football? _____

Speaker B: Do you like football? _____

2 🌐 40 **Listen and repeat the questions. Sound interested.**

a) What did you do today?

b) Did you go to school in England?

c) Where did you go on holiday?

d) Do you have any chocolate?

e) Are you interested in sharks?

f) Do you want to go out tonight?

Writing

Describing a holiday

1   **Read the email about a holiday. Answer the questions.**

   a)   Where did Clare go?
        South Africa

   b)   When did she go there?
        _____

   c)   Who did she go with?
        _____

   d)   How did she get there?
        _____

   e)   Where did she stay?
        _____

   f)   What did she do?
        _____

   g)   What interesting things did she see?
        _____

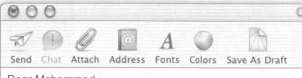

Dear Mohammed

Thanks for your email. I'm sorry I didn't reply, but I was on holiday. I went to South Africa last month for ten days. I went with my friends, Frank and Cassie. Do you remember them?

South Africa was fantastic! We went by plane to Cape Town. It's a great city. The mountains and the sea were so beautiful. We stayed in a really nice, small hotel by the sea. There's a lot to do in Cape Town, and the people are friendly. We went to some very good restaurants. We saw whales and went swimming with dolphins. I would love to go back there!

Write soon.

Love,
Clare

2   **Look at the email again and write the adjectives Clare uses to describe these things.**

   a)   South Africa   *fantastic*

   b)   Cape Town   _____

   c)   the mountains and the sea   _____

   d)   the hotel   _____

   e)   the people   _____

   f)   some restaurants   _____

3   **Write answers to the questions about your last holiday.**

   a)   Where did you go?
        _____

   b)   When did you go there?
        _____

   c)   Who did you go with?
        _____

   d)   How did you get there?
        _____

   e)   Where did you stay?
        _____

   f)   What did you do?
        _____

   g)   What interesting things did you see?
        _____

4   **Write an email to a friend about your last holiday. Use the notes you made in Exercise 3 to help you. Use some adjectives from Exercise 2.**

Grammar

1 **Complete the sentences with *There's* or *There are*.**

a) ____*There's*____ a TV in the bathroom.

b) _____ two sofas in the living room.

c) _____ some cushions on the sofa.

d) _____ a rug in the kitchen.

e) _____ some plants on the coffee table.

f) _____ a lamp on my desk.

g) _____ some books in the cupboard.

h) _____ four people in my family.

2 **Complete the sentences with *a, some* or *any*.**

a) There's ___*a*___ carpet in the bedroom.

b) There aren't _____ books in the bathroom.

c) There are _____ plants in the living room.

d) There aren't _____ books in the cupboard.

e) There's _____ cooker in the kitchen.

f) There are _____ cushions on the sofa.

3 **Write questions with *Is there ...?* or *Are there ...?***

a) chairs / in the kitchen?

   Are there any chairs in the kitchen?

b) mirror / in the living room?

   _____

c) cupboards / in the kitchen?

   _____

d) book / on the table?

   _____

e) cushions / on the sofa?

   _____

f) cooker / in the kitchen?

   _____

g) plants / in the kitchen?

   _____

h) plants / in the living room?

   _____

4 **Look at the pictures and write short answers to the questions in Exercise 3.**

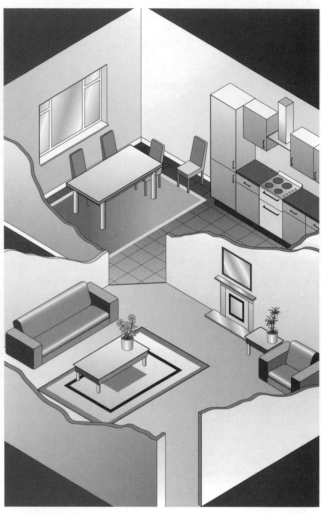

a) *Yes, there are.* _____

b) _____

c) _____

d) _____

e) _____

f) _____

g) _____

h) _____

5 **Complete the sentences to make them true for you.**

a) There's _____ in my kitchen.

b) There are _____ in the living room.

c) There isn't _____ in my home.

d) There aren't _____ in the bathroom.

Vocabulary

1 Label the rooms and the items in the pictures.

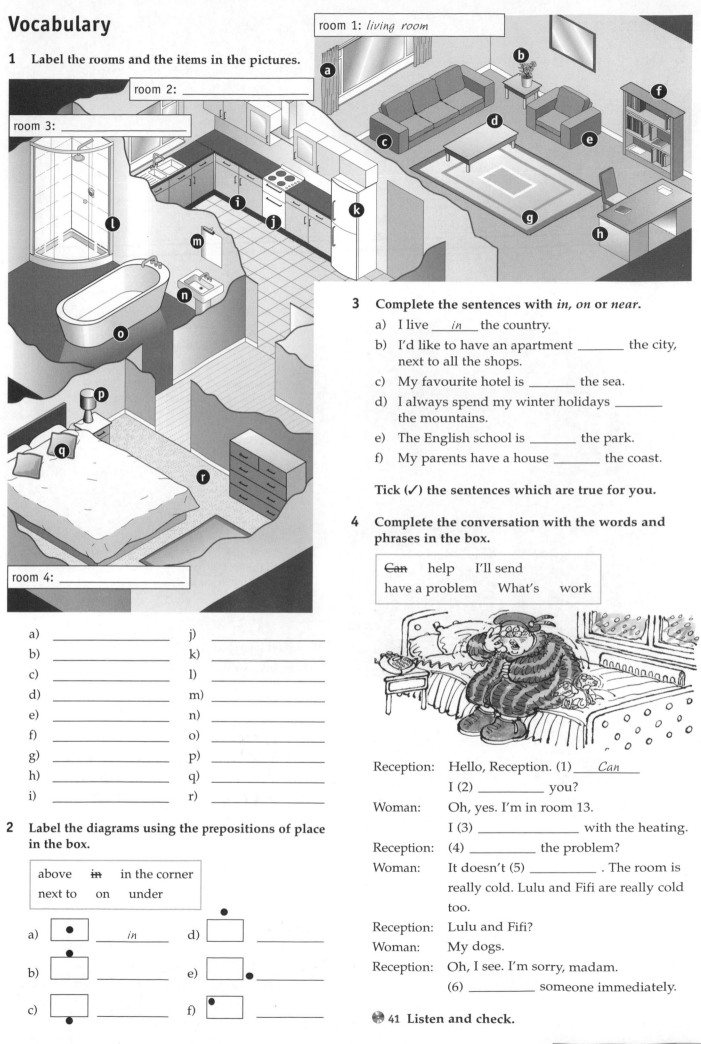

room 1: *living room*

room 2: _____

room 3: _____

room 4: _____

a) _____   j) _____
b) _____   k) _____
c) _____   l) _____
d) _____   m) _____
e) _____   n) _____
f) _____   o) _____
g) _____   p) _____
h) _____   q) _____
i) _____   r) _____

2 Label the diagrams using the prepositions of place in the box.

| above ~~in~~ in the corner |
| next to on under |

a) _____ *in* _____   d) _____

b) _____   e) _____

c) _____   f) _____

3 Complete the sentences with *in*, *on* or *near*.

a) I live ___*in*___ the country.

b) I'd like to have an apartment _____ the city, next to all the shops.

c) My favourite hotel is _____ the sea.

d) I always spend my winter holidays _____ the mountains.

e) The English school is _____ the park.

f) My parents have a house _____ the coast.

Tick (✓) the sentences which are true for you.

4 Complete the conversation with the words and phrases in the box.

| ~~Can~~ help I'll send |
| have a problem What's work |

Reception: Hello, Reception. (1)___*Can*___ I (2) _____ you?

Woman: Oh, yes. I'm in room 13. I (3) _____ with the heating.

Reception: (4) _____ the problem?

Woman: It doesn't (5) _____ . The room is really cold. Lulu and Fifi are really cold too.

Reception: Lulu and Fifi?

Woman: My dogs.

Reception: Oh, I see. I'm sorry, madam. (6) _____ someone immediately.

🔵 41 Listen and check.

Listening

1 Label the pictures with the words in the box.

balcony	concierge	fridge	phone
plants	shower	TV	washing machine

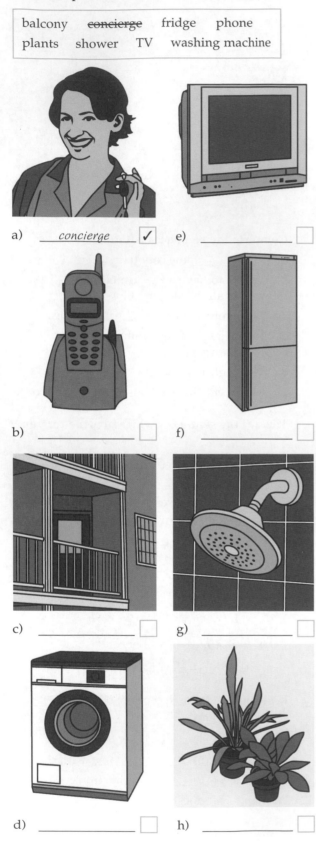

a) _concierge_ ✓   e) _____ ☐

b) _____ ☐   f) _____ ☐

c) _____ ☐   g) _____ ☐

d) _____ ☐   h) _____ ☐

2 🔵 42 **Cover the listening script. Listen and tick (✓) the items in Exercise 1 in Pam's flat.**

Pam: Hello?

Bea: Hi, Pam.

Pam: Oh, hi, Bea. Listen, I'm really happy that you want to stay in the flat this summer.

Bea: Me too. I have some questions about that, Pam. Do you have time?

Pam: Sure. What do you want to know?

Bea: OK, how big is the flat? You know, how many rooms does it have?

Pam: It's small. There are four rooms: a bedroom, a bathroom – with a shower, not a bath – a living room and a kitchen. Oh, and a balcony.

Bea: A balcony? Lovely. Is there a nice view?

Pam: You can see the sea. It's beautiful.

Bea: Great. And the kitchen – does it have a fridge?

Pam: Yes, fridge, cooker and washing machine.

Bea: And is there anything I have to remember to do? Are there any plants that need water?

Pam: No, there aren't any plants. And there aren't any phones in the building, either, so remember to take your mobile.

Bea: Oh, right.

Pam: Oh, and no TV, so take your computer, and some DVDs.

Bea: Yes, good idea.

Pam: The flat's in the city centre, so there are lots of shops near you.

Bea: Great. One last question – where's the key?

Pam: Oh, yes. The key. The concierge keeps the keys to all the flats. She can help you with any problems, as well. I hope you have a great time.

Bea: Thanks, Pam. I'm really excited.

3 Listen again and <u>underline</u> the correct answer.

a) Bea wants to stay in Pam's flat this <u>**summer**</u> / **winter**.

b) Pam's flat is **big** / **small**.

c) You can see the **mountains** / **sea** from the balcony.

d) There isn't a **TV** / **fridge** in Pam's flat.

e) The flat is in the **city** / **country**.

f) **Pam** / **The concierge** has the key to the flat.

4 Listen again. Are the statements true (T) or false (F)?

a) Pam wants Bea to stay in her flat. __T__

b) The flat has four bedrooms. _____

c) There's a shower in the flat but there isn't a bath. _____

d) There's a computer in the flat. _____

e) There aren't any shops near the flat. _____

f) The concierge can help Bea with any problems. _____

Writing

Describing your home and the area near it

1 Read the note. Tick (✓) the questions below that the note answers.

Dear Dominic

Welcome! The first thing is the key. Go to Number 23. My friend Katia lives there. She has the key.

The house has three bedrooms, two bathrooms, a living room and kitchen. And there's a big garden at the back. I think it's perfect for you and your family.

There are some shops near the house. The supermarket is open until ten every evening. There's a park near the house and there's a railway station next to the park. Trains into the city centre go every 20 minutes.

If you have any problems, ask Katia – she's a good friend. Hope you have a lovely time!

Love from Gabi

a) How many rooms are there? ✓
b) Does it have a balcony?
c) Is there a washing machine?
d) Are there any shops near the house?
e) Is it near a park?
f) Is it near a train station?
g) Is it in the city centre?
h) Are there any problems with the flat?

2 A friend wants to stay in your home. Write notes to answer the questions in Exercise 1 about your home. Add more information about your home.

Example

4 rooms — bedroom, bathroom, kitchen, living room

_____

_____

_____

_____

_____

3 Write a note to your friend. Tell him/her about your home and the area around your home. Use the notes you made in Exercise 2 to help you.

Pronunciation

1 🌐 43 Listen to the sounds /s/ and /ʃ/.

/s/ <u>c</u>entre

/ʃ/ <u>ch</u>andelier

2 🌐 44 Listen to the words in the box. Is the <u>underlined</u> sound /s/ or /ʃ/? Put the words in the correct column.

| ~~<u>c</u>entre~~ ~~<u>ch</u>andelier~~ cu<u>sh</u>ions paradi<u>s</u>e |
| pea<u>c</u>e pla<u>c</u>e <u>s</u>eaplane <u>sh</u>ampoo <u>sh</u>ower |
| spa<u>ci</u>ous spe<u>ci</u>al stre<u>ss</u> <u>s</u>uite wa<u>sh</u>basin |

/s/	/ʃ/
centre	*chandelier*

🌐 45 Listen and check. Repeat the words.

10 Food

Grammar

1 Find the food words in the wordsnake and write them in the correct column.

potato bread cheese olive oil mushroom grape orange carrot cereal garlic

Countable nouns	Uncountable nouns
potato	

2 Complete the conversation with *a*, *any* or *some*.

WHAT'S IN THE BAG?

Presenter: Welcome to *What's in the Bag?* Remember, you take home the items you guess correctly.

May: Is there (1) _any_ butter?

Presenter: No. There's (2) _____ margarine, but there isn't (3) _____ butter.

May: Is there (4) _____ pear?

Presenter: No. There's (5) _____ banana, but there isn't (6) _____ pear.

May: Oh, dear. Are there (7) _____ tomatoes?

Presenter: No. There are (8) _____ potatoes, but there aren't (9) _____ tomatoes.

May: Is there (10) _____ cheese?

Presenter: Yes, there is. We have a winner!

🌐 46 **Listen and check.**

3 Complete the conversation with *is*, *isn't*, *are* or *aren't*.

Di: Jem, it's me. I'm in the supermarket. Could you look in the kitchen? (1) _Are_ there any tomatoes?

Jem: Yes, there (2) _____ .

Di: Oh, great. And (3) _____ there any bread?

Jem: No, there (4) _____ .

Di: Oh, all right. (5) _____ there any bananas?

Jem: Um, no, there (6) _____ .

Di: OK, thanks. That's all. Oh no, one more thing. (7) _____ there any pasta?

Jem: Yes, there (8) _____ .

Di: Thanks, darling. See you later.

🌐 47 **Listen and check.**

4 <u>Underline</u> the correct word.

a) How **much** / <u>**many**</u> oranges are there?

b) How **much** / **many** cheese is there?

c) How **much** / **many** grapes are there?

d) How **much** / **many** milk is there?

e) How **much** / **many** rice there?

f) How **much** / **many** potatoes are there?

5 Look at the picture and match the answers (*1–6*) with the questions in Exercise 4 (*a–f*).

1 There isn't much. _d_

2 There are a lot. _____

3 There aren't any. _____

4 There's a lot. _____

5 There isn't any. _____

6 There aren't many. _____

Vocabulary

1 Look at the pictures and complete the crossword.

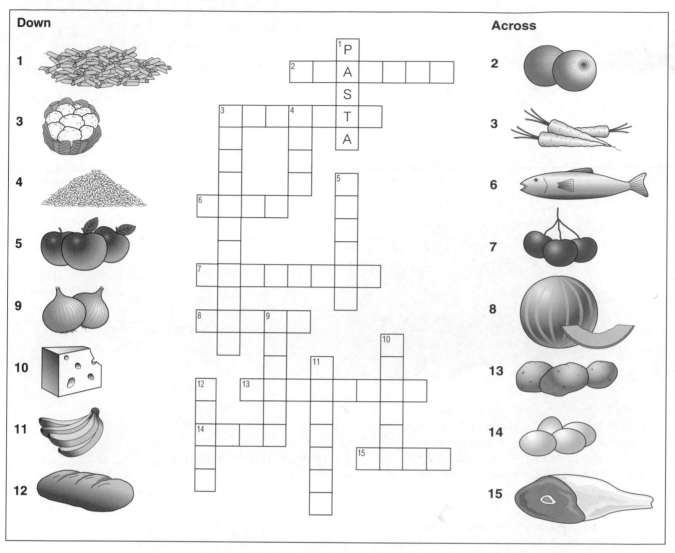

Down

1
3
4
5
9
10
11
12

Across

2
3
6
7
8
13
14
15

2 Put the words in Exercise 1 in the correct column.

Carbohydrate	Protein	Vegetable	Fruit
pasta			

3 <u>Underline</u> the odd word out.

a) beans <u>cheese</u> mushrooms peppers

b) grape lemon strawberry garlic

c) pears cakes cereal bread

d) seafood meat pasta fish

4 Complete the conversation with the words in the box.

| anything | black | brown | ~~like~~ |
| That's | Would | you | |

Customer: I'd (1) ___*like*___ a steak sandwich, please.

Assistant: (2) _____ you like white or (3) _____ bread?

Customer: White, please.

Assistant: Would (4) _____ like any onions?

Customer: Yes, please.

Assistant: Would you like (5) _____ to drink?

Customer: Yes. A coffee, please.

Assistant: White or (6) _____ ?

Customer: White, please.

Assistant: (7) _____ £8, please.

Customer: Thanks.

🔊 **48** Listen and check.

Reading

1 **Read the article and answer the question.**

Where does the Mediterranean diet come from?

_____

In the 1960s, an American scientist, Ancel Keys, wanted to know why people in some countries live longer than people in other countries. Keys studied the diets of 13,000 men, aged 40–59, in seven countries. He found that the diet on the Greek island of Crete was the healthiest. He called this healthy diet 'the Mediterranean diet'.

Here is how you can eat a healthy Mediterranean diet, like the people of Crete.

- Eat 20–30 portions of fruit and vegetables a week.
- Don't eat a lot of butter.
- Eat more 'good' fats like olive oil.
- Eat fish and chicken.
- Don't eat a lot of red meat.
- Drink red wine with meals.
- Don't eat more than four eggs a week.
- Don't eat food with a lot of sugar in it, like biscuits and cakes.
- Eat more beans.
- Bread is OK, but without butter.
- Don't eat a lot of potatoes.

The important thing is to eat a healthy mix of different types of food every day. And remember – enjoy your food!

2 <u>Underline</u> **the correct answer.**

a) Ancel Keys studied <u>**men**</u> / **women** in seven countries.

b) The Mediterranean diet **has a lot of** / **doesn't have much** fruit.

c) Olive oil is **good** / **bad** for you.

d) People on Crete drink wine **in the morning** / **with their food**.

e) Biscuits and cakes have a lot of **sugar** / **eggs** in them.

f) It's important to eat a lot of **beans** / **different types of food** every day.

3 **Read the article again. Are the statements true (T) or false (F)?**

a) Ancel Keys did the diet study because he wanted to know why some people were fat.
   _F_

b) Butter is a 'good' fat. _____

c) There isn't much red meat in the Mediterranean diet. _____

d) People on Crete eat eggs every day. _____

e) There isn't much sugar in the Mediterranean diet. _____

f) People on Crete never eat bread. _____

g) Beans are an important part of the Mediterranean diet. _____

Pronunciation

1 🔘 **49 Listen to the sounds /ɪ/ and /iː/.**

/ɪ/   ch<u>i</u>cken

/iː/   b<u>ea</u>ns

2 🔘 **50 Listen to the words in the box. Is the <u>underlined</u> sound /ɪ/ or /iː/? Put the words in the correct column.**

~~beans~~	ch<u>ee</u>se	~~chicken~~	ch<u>i</u>ps	d<u>i</u>fferent
<u>ea</u>t	f<u>i</u>sh	garl<u>i</u>c	l<u>i</u>st	l<u>i</u>ve	m<u>ea</u>t
n<u>ee</u>d	prot<u>ei</u>n	s<u>ea</u>food

/ɪ/	/iː/
chicken	_beans_
_____	_____
_____	_____
_____	_____
_____	_____
_____	_____
_____	_____

🔘 **51 Listen and check. Repeat the words.**

Writing

Writing an invitation

1 Look at the two invitations and answer the questions.

   a) Which invitation is written in a formal, serious style? ____

   b) Which invitation is written in an informal, friendly style to someone the sender knows well? ____

> ### *Invitation*   **1**
>
> *Mr and Mrs Gregg invite you to a party*
> *to celebrate the graduation of their son, James*
> **Riverside House, the Ridings, Sprotton**
>
> Friday 14th July
> 9 p.m. – midnight
>
> RSVP

> **2**
>
> Dear Chantal
>
> Can you and Tom come to lunch on Sunday? It's my birthday. Come at about 12 o'clock. My new address is Flat 2, Park Villas, Gadd Street.
>
> Hope you can come. Call me this week!
> Love, Kristy

2 Read the invitations again, and answer the questions.

   a) What is the event?

Invitation 1   *a party*

Invitation 2 _____

   b) Who is the event for?

Invitation 1 _____

Invitation 2 _____

   c) Where is the event?

Invitation 1 _____

Invitation 2 _____

   d) What's the date of the event?

Invitation 1 _____

Invitation 2 _____

   e) What time does it start?

Invitation 1 _____

Invitation 2 _____

   f) What expression is used to ask people to reply to the invitation?

Invitation 1 _____

Invitation 2 _____

3 Imagine you want to invite people to a formal and informal event. Make notes.

   a) What is the event?

formal _____

informal _____

   b) Who is the event for?

formal _____

informal _____

   c) Where is the event?

formal _____

informal _____

   d) When is the date of the event?

formal _____

informal _____

   e) What time does it start?

formal _____

informal _____

4 Write your invitations. Use the invitations in Exercise 1 and the notes you made in Exercise 3 to help you.

11 Looks

Grammar

1 Complete the sentences with the present continuous form of the verbs in the box.

~~have~~	make	sing	sit	wear	work

a) He *'s having* lunch.

b) My aunt _____ a very big hat.

c) I _____ here.

d) They _____ sad songs.

e) We _____ a cake.

f) You _____ too fast.

2 Write questions in the present continuous.

a) your father / read / this book?
Is your father reading this book?

b) it / rain?
_____

c) your friends / make a noise outside?
_____

d) I / stand on your foot?
_____

e) we/ earn a lot of money?
_____

f) she / wear a black top?
_____

3 Write short answers to the questions in Exercise 2.

a) Yes, *he is.*
b) No, _____
c) Yes, _____
d) No, you _____
e) Yes, we _____
f) No, _____

4 Write questions with *you* in the present continuous.

a) What / do
What are you doing?

b) What / wear
_____

c) Where / sit
_____

d) drink / cup of coffee
_____

e) have / a good time
_____

5 Write true answers for the questions in Exercise 4.

Example (a)
I'm watching TV.

a) _____
b) _____
c) _____
d) _____
e) _____

Vocabulary

1 **Label the pictures with the words in the box.**

~~belt~~	boots	hat	jacket	jeans	
shirt	shoes	skirt	suit	sunglasses	sweater
tie	top	trainers	trousers	T-shirt	

a) _____belt_____ i) _____
b) _____ j) _____
c) _____ k) _____
d) _____ l) _____
e) _____ m) _____
f) _____ n) _____
g) _____ o) _____
h) _____ p) _____

2 **Are the words in Exercise 1 singular or plural nouns? Write *S* or *P* next to each word.**

a) _____belt S_____

3 **Put the words in Exercise 1 in groups.**

Footwear
___boots___ _____ _____

Formal clothes
_____ _____ _____

_____ _____ _____

Casual clothes
_____ _____ _____

Accessories
_____ _____ _____

4 **Complete the descriptions of the people with the words in the box.**

beard	blond	eyes	good-looking
lovely	smile	~~short~~	

My brother David has (1) _____short_____ ,
(2) _____ hair and green
(3) _____ . He has a (4) _____
and a moustache. I don't think he's very
(5) _____ , but he has a
(6) _____ !

brown	medium-length	straight	sweet

My daughter Ruby is very (7) _____ .
She has (8) _____ , (9) _____ ,
brown hair and (10) _____ eyes.

5 **Complete the conversation with the words in the box.**

about	changing rooms	colour	have
~~help~~	looking	special	try

Assistant: Can I (1) _____help_____ you?

Customer: No, I'm just (2) _____ , thanks.

Assistant: Are you looking for anything
(3) _____ ?

Customer: Well, yes. I'm looking for a winter coat.

Assistant: What (4) _____ are you looking
for?

Customer: Black or brown, I think.

Assistant: How (5) _____ this grey one?

Customer: Hmm, grey. I like it. Do you
(6) _____ it in a small?

Assistant: Yes. Here you are.

Customer: Can I (7) _____ it on?

Assistant: Yes. The (8) _____ are
over there.

🔵 52 **Listen and check.**

Listening

1 🔘 53 **Cover the listening script. Listen to the conversation between Sacha and Zoë. Which of the following *didn't* happen?**

a) Sacha made a phone call.

b) Sacha saw Brad Pitt.

c) Sacha talked to a woman with big earrings.

d) Brad Pitt smiled at Sacha.

2 **Listen again and <u>underline</u> the correct answers.**

a) Sacha is at **a restaurant** / <u>**an airport**</u>.

b) Sacha is wearing a **pink top** / **pink hat**.

c) Brad Pitt arrived **before** / **after** Sacha.

d) Brad Pitt is talking to **other actors** / **the fans**.

e) The woman with the tattoos is wearing big **sunglasses** / **earrings**.

f) Brad Pitt is wearing a pair of **jeans** / **trainers**.

3 **Listen again. Are the statements true (T) or false (F)?**

a) Sacha thinks Brad Pitt is good-looking.
   _T_

b) Sacha and Zoë are together. _____

c) Sacha is wearing black trousers. _____

d) Sacha is wearing a black hat. _____

e) Sacha likes the woman Brad Pitt is talking to. _____

f) Brad Pitt is wearing a suit and sunglasses.
   _____

Sacha:	Zoë? It's me, Sacha.
Zoë:	Hi, Sacha. Where are you?
Sacha:	I'm here at the airport. I'm waiting to meet my sister. And guess what – Brad Pitt's on her flight!
Zoë:	No!
Sacha:	Yeah!
Zoë:	Is he there?
Sacha:	Not yet.
Zoë:	What are you wearing?
Sacha:	I'm in my pink top with my black trousers and my long, brown boots. Oh, and I'm wearing my black hat.
Zoë:	Beautiful!
Sacha:	Oh, yes! Here he is! Oh, Zoë, he's really handsome!
Zoë:	Oh. What's he doing?
Sacha:	He's talking to some fans. Oh, urgh!
Zoë:	What?
Sacha:	He's talking to a woman in a very small dress with tattoos and big earrings. She looks terrible!
Zoë:	Urgh! Anyway, what's *he* wearing?
Sacha:	He's wearing a suit, a dark shirt and sunglasses. Oh, and a really cool pair of trainers.
Zoë:	Lovely!
Sacha:	Uh-oh. Zoë, he's smiling at me.
Zoë:	What?
Sacha:	He's coming over here.
Zoë:	Sacha? Sach?

Pronunciation

1 🔘 54 **Listen and repeat the numbers.**

13 14 15 16 17 18 19

30 40 50 60 70 80 90

2 🔘 55 **Listen and circle the number you hear.**

a) 13 ⃝30

b) 14 40

c) 15 50

d) 16 60

e) 17 70

f) 18 80

g) 19 90

Writing

Linking sentences: *and, with*
Describing a person

A

1 She's a young woman.
2 She has long, blonde hair.
3 She has green eyes.
4 She's wearing a formal evening dress.
5 She's very beautiful.

B

She's a young woman with long, blonde hair and green eyes. She's wearing a formal evening dress and she's very beautiful.

1 Read the descriptions in *A* and *B* and answer the questions.

a) How many sentences are there in *A*?

b) How many sentences are there in *B*?

c) Which word in *B* links sentences *1* and *2* from *A*?

d) Which word in *B* links sentences *2* and *3* from *A*?

e) Which word in *B* links sentences *4* and *5* from *A*?

2 Complete the description of Orlando Bloom.

1 Orlando Bloom is a _____*young*_____ man.
(age adjective)

2 He has _____ hair.
(length and colour adjective)

3 He has _____ eyes.
(colour adjective)

4 He has _____ .
(accessories or other, e.g. moustache)

5 He's wearing _____ clothes.
(style adjective)

6 He's _____ .
(opinion)

3 Rewrite the six sentences in Exercise 2 as three sentences. Use *with* and *and* to link the sentences.

_____

_____

_____

_____

_____

4 Choose a person to describe. Write six sentences.

1 _____

2 _____

3 _____

4 _____

5 _____

6 _____

5 Write a description of the person you chose. Use the sentences you wrote in Exercise 4 to help you. Use *with* and *and* to link the sentences.

_____

_____

_____

_____

_____

12 Money

Grammar

1 Write the comparative form of the adjectives.

Short adjectives	Comparative form
clean	*cleaner*
fast	_____
old	_____
tall	_____
cheap	_____
short	_____
young	_____
ugly	_____

Long adjectives

beautiful	_____
interesting	_____
expensive	_____
famous	_____

Irregular adjectives

good	_____
bad	_____
far	_____

2 Complete the sentences with comparative adjectives from Exercise 1.

I'm 26.

I'm 16.

a) The man is _____*older*_____ than the boy.

b) The boy is _____ than the man.

£500

£5

c) The TV is _____ than the book.

d) The book is _____ than the TV.

e) The woman is _____ than the man.

f) The man is _____ than the woman.

g) Leo's painting is _____ than Dino's.

h) Dino's painting is _____ than Leo's.

3 Complete the sentences with the superlative form of the adjectives (in brackets).

a) Luxembourg is _____*the richest*_____ (rich) country in the world.

b) _____ (expensive) mobile phone in the world costs £500,000.

c) Mothers have _____ (important) job in the world.

d) Pelé is _____ (good) footballer of all time.

e) Rajshahi in Bangladesh is _____ (happy) city in the world.

f) Russia is _____ (big) country in the world.

4 Complete the sentences with the superlative form of the adjectives in the box.

famous	~~fast~~	old	tall	valuable	young

a) The cheetah is _____*the fastest*_____ animal.

b) At 508 metres, Taipei 101 is _____ building in the world.

c) 10-year-old Tatum O'Neal was _____ person to win an Oscar.

d) Bologna has _____ university in the world. It opened in 1088.

e) At $1.65 million, the Diamond-fruit Cake is _____ cake in the world.

f) The Mona Lisa is _____ painting in the world.

Vocabulary

1 **Find the words connected with money in the wordsnake.**

savebuyearnspenddebtsalarybillscredit

a) _____save_____   e) _____

b) _____   f) _____

c) _____   g) _____

d) _____   h) _____

2 **Complete the text with the words in Exercise 1.**

Hi

My name's Darren. I need your help. I have a
(1) _____debt_____ of $3,000, and it's getting bigger.
I have a job, but my company doesn't pay me
enough. My (2) _____ is $18,000 but I really
need to (3) _____ $30,000. Life here is
expensive. I (4) _____ my money on food and
accommodation. I pay all of my
(5) _____ on time. But I can't (6) _____
any money because at the end of the month there's
nothing left. It was bad before and now it's worse. I
can only (7) _____ things on my (8) _____
card. Can you help me?

🌐 **56 Listen and check.**

3 **Write the prices in words.**

a) $3,276,530

three million, two hundred and seventy-six
thousand, five hundred and thirty dollars

b) $724,115

_____

_____

_____

c) $499,130

_____

_____

_____

d) $13,194,720

_____

_____

_____

4 **Write the prices in numbers.**

a) Thirty-nine thousand, six hundred and ten
dollars.

_$39,610_____

b) Twelve million, seven hundred and eighty-five
thousand, two hundred and twenty dollars.

_____

c) Seventy-eight thousand, two hundred and
ninety dollars.

_____

d) One million, one hundred and forty-five
thousand, eight hundred and fifty-nine dollars.

_____

e) Eight hundred and nineteen thousand, four
hundred and forty dollars.

_____

f) Two hundred and twelve thousand, three
hundred and fifty dollars.

_____

5 **Complete the conversation with the words in the box.**

anything	brown	good
handbag	~~kind~~	leather

Son: Is everything OK?

Mum: No, I can't find my bag.

Son: What (1) _____kind_____ of bag is it?

Mum: A (2) _____ .

Son: Is there (3) _____ in it?

Mum: Yes, my money and my mobile phone.

Son: Is it a sort of dark (4) _____
colour?

Mum: Yes.

Son: Is it made of (5) _____ ?

Mum: Yes, that's it.

Son: Sorry. I don't know.

Mum: Oh, Kyle!

Son: Why don't you call your mobile and listen
for the noise?

Mum: Oh, that's a (6) _____ idea.

🌐 **57 Listen and check.**

Reading

1 🌐 **58 Read the text and look at the bar chart and answer the question.**

Who spent/spends more on eating out?

a) People a hundred years ago

b) People today

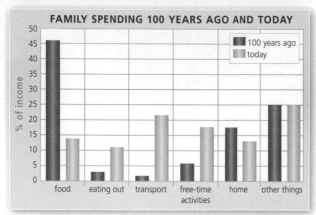

FAMILY SPENDING 100 YEARS AGO AND TODAY

Researchers looked at the spending habits of families in the USA one hundred years ago and today.

These were the biggest differences the researchers found.

A hundred years ago people spent more on food. This is because food was very expensive and families were bigger. Food is cheaper today, and people have smaller families. But people eat out in restaurants a lot more today.

People spend more on transport today than they did a hundred years ago. This is because people today have cars or travel to work on trains and buses.

People a hundred years ago didn't spend a lot on free-time activities. Today families spend more on free-time activities and holidays.

Life a hundred years ago was more difficult and people were more careful with money than today.

2 **Look at the bar chart again and complete the sentences.**

a) People a hundred years ago spent most of their money on ____food____ .

b) People today spend more on eating out, _____ and free-time activities.

c) People a hundred years ago spent _____ per cent (%) of their money on food.

d) People today spend nearly twenty per cent (%) of their money on _____ .

e) People one hundred years ago spent _____ on their home than people today.

f) People today and people a hundred years ago spent the same on _____ things.

3 **Read the text again. Are the statements true (T) or false (F)? Correct the false statements.**

a) The survey studied the spending habits of people a hundred years ago and people today.
    T _____

b) The people in the survey lived in the UK.
    _____

c) People a hundred years ago spent more on food than people today.
    _____

d) Families today are bigger than they were a hundred years ago.
    _____

e) People today spend less on transport than people a hundred years ago.
    _____

f) Life today is easier than life a hundred years ago.
    _____

Pronunciation

🌐 **59 Listen to the words and cross out the 'silent' letters.**

a) lis~~t~~en

b) debt

c) wrote

d) handsome

e) cupboard

f) interesting

g) different

h) two

Listen again and repeat the words.

Writing

Writing a summary of graphic data

1 Look at the bar chart opposite. Complete the summary with the phrases in the box.

> A surprising thing is ~~The chart shows~~ After that
>
> The second highest thing is
>
> spends more on spends most on

Family weekly spending in the today.

(1) _The chart shows_ the weekly spending of families in the UK. The average British family

(2) _____ transport.

(3) _____ leisure and culture. (4) _____ comes food, then housing and electricity.

(5) _____ that the average family

(6) _____ alcohol and cigarettes than on health.

2 Look at the bar chart opposite and answer the questions.

a) What does the chart show?

Yearly spending of people in the US.

b) What does the average American person spend most on?

_____

c) What's the second highest thing?

_____

d) What is the most surprising thing?

_____

3 Write a summary of the information given in the chart. Use the answers to the questions in Exercise 2 to help you.

_____
_____
_____
_____
_____
_____
_____
_____
_____
_____
_____
_____

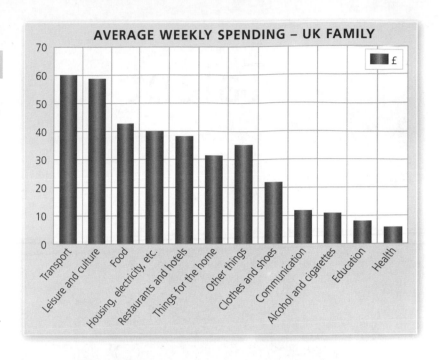

AVERAGE WEEKLY SPENDING – UK FAMILY

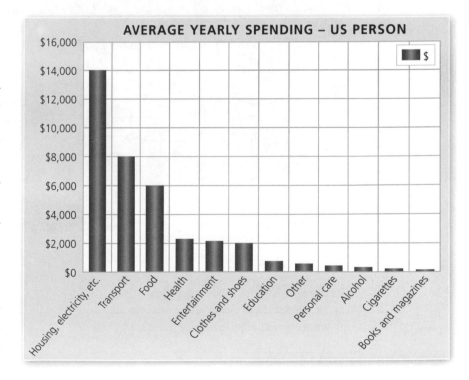

AVERAGE YEARLY SPENDING – US PERSON

13 Talent

Grammar

1 Complete the sentences with *can* and *can't* and the verbs in the box.

| ~~dance~~ | drive | ski | swim | talk | walk |

a) They _can't dance_ .

d) I _____

b) He _____

e) It _____

c) We _____

f) You _____

2 Write questions with *can*.

a) you / play football?

Can you play football?

b) your teacher / speak Italian?

_____

c) you / cook?

_____

d) your parents / ski?

_____

e) you / sing?

_____

f) you and your friends / dance?

_____

3 Write true short answers to the questions in Exercise 2.

Example (a)

Yes, I can.

a) _____

b) _____

c) _____

d) _____

e) _____

f) _____

4 Complete the table.

Adjective	Adverb
bad	*badly*
good	
careful	
happy	
fast	
loud	
quiet	
slow	

5 Write sentences with the adverb in the correct position.

a) (slow) You / always eat / so

You always eat so slowly.

b) (fast) Isabella / talk / very

_____

c) (good) My sister / sing / really

_____

d) (careful) Ken / do / his work

_____

e) (loud) They / talk / very

_____

f) (bad) I / swim / very

_____

6 Put the frequency expressions in order.

~~all the time~~	Frequent	_all the time_
every day	↑	_____
every year		_____
never		_____
once a month	↓	_____
twice a day	Not frequent	_____

Vocabulary

1 Find the adjectives in the wordsnake.

confident generous selfish sensible serious shy

a) _____confident_____

b) _____

c) _____

d) _____

e) _____

f) _____

2 Complete the sentences with an adjective from Exercise 1.

a) Ben is a very _____generous_____ person. He often buys me lunch, and he sometimes gives money to his friends.

b) My sister often gets nervous when she meets new people. She's quite _____ .

c) Our father is always _____ . He thinks carefully before he does anything, and he never does stupid things!

d) I don't like Camilla! She's always thinks about herself and she never thinks about me. She's so _____ .

e) Why is Ludovik so _____ ? He never laughs when I say something funny.

f) Your boyfriend is very _____ and sure of himself.

3 Match the adjectives with their opposites in the box.

| quiet | confident | serious |
| stupid | unfriendly | |

a) shy _____confident_____

b) friendly _____

c) funny _____

d) sensible _____

e) loud _____

4 Complete the conversation with the words in the box.

| about | bad | can't | have |
| money | time | tired | want |

John: Cathy, do you (1) _____want_____ to go out tonight?

Cathy: No, I just want to sit in a quiet room. I (2) _____ a terrible headache.

John: What (3) _____ tomorrow?

Cathy: Maybe.

John: Do you want to go shopping on Saturday, Rosa?

Rosa: I want to, but I don't have any (4) _____ .

John: Hey, Mark, do you want to go swimming tomorrow?

Mark: No, I (5) _____ . I have a cold.

John: Do you want to go to the cinema with me later, Dan?

Dan: Not tonight. I'm really (6) _____ . I'm going to bed.

John: Gary, do you want to play football with us next week?

Gary: No, I have a (7) _____ back. But there's a great film on TV tonight. Do you want to watch it with me?

John: Sorry, I don't have (8) _____ .

🔊 60 **Listen and check.**

Reading

1 🔘 61 **Read the article. Complete the sentences with the names in the box.**

> Johnny Depp Keith Richards Ronnie Wood

a) _____ plays the part of Jack Sparrow's father in *Pirates of the Caribbean 3*.

b) _____ likes painting pictures of rock stars.

c) _____ played the guitar in the film *Chocolat*.

2 **Read the article again. Are the statements true (T) or false (F)?**

a) Johnny Depp's first film was *Platoon*. __F__

b) He directed the film *The Brave*. _____

c) Johnny Depp wrote the music for the song *Fade-In-Out*. _____

d) He played the guitar on a Rolling Stones song. _____

e) Keith Richards and Johnny Depp are in the film *Pirates of the Caribbean 3*. _____

f) Ronnie Wood and Keith Richards are in The Rolling Stones. _____

3 **Read the article again and <u>underline</u> the correct answers in the summary.**

Johnny Depp appeared in his first film in (1) **<u>1984</u> / 1986**. Then, (2) **three / thirteen** years later he directed his first film. He is a talented man and can play many (3) **sports / musical instruments**. He also writes (4) **music / books**. Rolling Stones guitarist (5) **Ronnie Wood / Keith Richards** is one of Depp's heroes. He plays the part of (6) **Wood's / Depp's** father in the film *Pirates of the Caribbean 3*. Another Rolling Stones guitarist, (7) **Ronnie Wood / Keith Richards**, is a talented painter.

Hidden talents

JOHNNY DEPP is a famous actor. His first film was *A Nightmare on Elm Street* in 1984 and then in 1986 he was in the film *Platoon*. Soon he became a teen hero.

But Johnny Depp is not only an actor, he is also a film director. In 1997 he directed and acted in the film *The Brave*. And Johnny Depp has hidden talents too. He can play many musical instruments and he can compose music. He played the guitar in the film *Chocolat* and on the song *Fade-In-Out* by British band Oasis. He also wrote some of the music in the film *Once Upon a Time in Mexico*.

One of Johnny Depp's favourite bands is The Rolling Stones and one of his heroes is Rolling Stones guitarist Keith Richards. In the film *Pirates of the Caribbean 3*, Richards shows his talent for acting. Johnny Depp plays the part of Jack Sparrow in the film, and Richards plays the part of his father. Ronnie Wood, another guitarist in The Rolling Stones, has a different talent – he can paint. He paints portraits of rock stars, including The Rolling Stones.

Pronunciation

1 🔘 62 **Listen to the pronunciation of the sound /ə/ in the <u>underlined</u> words.**

1 A: How many instruments <u>can</u> you play?
   B: Two. I <u>can</u> play the guitar and the piano.

2 A: What <u>do</u> you do?
   B: I'm <u>a</u> doctor.

3 A: Which languages <u>can</u> you speak?
   B: Spanish <u>and</u> English.

4 A: What <u>was</u> the last thing you bought?
   B: A pair <u>of</u> shoes.

2 🔘 63 **Listen again and repeat.**

Writing

Correcting mistakes with capital letters
and spelling
Writing about a talented person

1 Read the first draft of a text. There are five words
which need capital letters. Find them in the text
and <u>underline</u> them. Write the words below.

1 _____Neil_____

2 _____

3 _____

4 _____

5 _____

> The person I know (wiht) the most talent is my best
> friend, <u>neil</u>. He and I were at shool together.
>
> Neil can play the guiter, and he plays the drums in
> a band. The band made their first cd last yaer. He
> is a really good singer, too. And he dances really
> well. He's very good at sports. He swims 1,000
> metres every day, he goes skiing evry winter and
> sailing every sumer.
>
> He and his band went to rome last weak and
> played two concerts. He loves italy and the italian
> people. He's having a holiday there now.
>
> Neil is a great friend and a realy interesting man.

2 There are eight spelling mistakes in the text. Find
them and circle them. Write the correct words
below.

1 _____with_____

2 _____

3 _____

4 _____

5 _____

6 _____

7 _____

8 _____

3 Look again at the text in Exercise 1. Match each
paragraph with a question below.

a) What do you think of the person?

   Paragraph _____

b) Who is the person and how do you know them?

   Paragraph ___1___

c) What can the person do?

   Paragraph _____

d) What is the person doing at the moment?

   Paragraph _____

4 Think of a talented person you know. Answer the
questions in Exercise 3 in the correct order as your
first draft.

5 Check your first draft for spelling and capital
letters. Write your final draft.

14 TV

Grammar

1 Write the words in the correct order to make questions.

a) to   rich   you   one day   hope   Do   be   ?
   Do you hope to be rich one day?

b) hope   retire   do   to   you   When   ?
   _____

c) famous   to   be   Would   like   you   ?
   _____

d) want   get married   Do   to   you   ?
   _____

e) a foreign country   you   to   in   Do   live   want   ?
   _____

f) you   travel   to   Would   round the world   like   ?
   _____

2 Match the answers below with the questions from Exercise 1.

1 No, I don't. I like my country.   *e*

2 No, I wouldn't. I'm very shy.   _____

3 When I'm sixty.   _____

4 Not really. Money doesn't always make you happy.   _____

5 Yes, I would. I'd really like to see Patagonia, Java and the Sahara.   _____

6 Yes, I do. And then I'd like to have lots of children.   _____

3 Make questions with *(be) going to*.

a) What / you / do tomorrow?
   What are you going to do tomorrow?

b) What / you / buy tomorrow?
   _____

c) What / you / watch on TV tonight?
   _____

d) Who / you / see next weekend?
   _____

e) Where / you / go for your next holiday?
   _____

f) Who / you / meet tomorrow?
   _____

4 Write true answers to the questions in Exercise 3.

Example (a)

   I'm going to go to work.

a) _____
b) _____
c) _____
d) _____
e) _____
f) _____

5 Complete the sentences with the words or contractions in the box.

to   're   'd   's   not   don't   ~~'m~~

a) I   *'m*   going to have a party this Saturday.

b) My girlfriend _____ going to come.

c) I _____ want to invite my brother's friends.

d) I _____ like to dance all night.

e) I'm going _____ buy some new CDs tomorrow.

f) I'm _____ going to buy a lot of food.

g) We _____ going to have a great time.

Vocabulary

1 Complete the names of six kinds of TV show.

a) ch<u>a</u>t sh<u>o</u>w

b) d_c_m_nt_r_y

c) g_m_ sh_w

d) th_ n_ws

e) r__l_ty TV sh_w

f) s__p _p_r_

2 Read the clues and write the type of show from Exercise 1 in the crossword.

Down

1 **Jonathan Ross**
Jonathan interviews the stars of cinema, pop music and TV.

3 **Wife Swap**
Show in which two wives live with each other's family for two weeks.

4 **Who Wants to be a Millionaire?**
Contestants answer questions and try to win a million pounds.

Across

2 **Neighbours**
More stories in the daily lives of the people of Melbourne, Australia.

5 **BBC One O'Clock Headlines**
The latest information about what's happening around the world.

6 **March of the Penguins**
Film about the long journey penguins make every year.

3 Complete the text with the words in the box.

channels	on	programme	switch
~~television~~	watch		

I don't have a (1) ___television___ in my house. If there's a (2) _____ I'm interested in, I (3) _____ on my computer and (4) _____ it on that. The computer is fantastic. The picture is great and when I want to find out what's (5) _____ , I check the online TV guide. It's much faster than looking for the TV magazine. And online there are more (6) _____ than on normal TV, so there are more programmes to choose from.

🔘 **64 Listen and check.**

4 Complete the conversation with the words in the box.

choose	I'll	Let's	on	Shall	stay
tired	~~want~~	watch			

Donna: What do you (1) ___want___ to do tonight?

Rick: I'm (2) _____ . I don't want to do anything. Shall we (3) _____ at home and (4) _____ TV?

Donna: OK. What's (5) _____ ?

Rick: Mm, nothing really.

Donna: (6) _____ we get a DVD?

Rick: Good idea. (7) _____ get a pizza, too, and have a relaxing evening.

Donna: Great. (8) _____ call for the pizza and you (9) _____ a film.

🔘 **65 Listen and check.**

Listening

1 🌀 66 Cover the listening script. Listen. Who is Lucy?

_____

2 Listen again. Are the statements true (T) or false (F)?

a) Darren won two million pounds. __F__

b) Darren is a bus driver. _____

c) Lucy loves travelling. _____

d) Darren is going to buy a big house. _____

e) Darren doesn't want to change his life. _____

f) Darren is going to spend all the money. _____

3 Answer the questions.

a) Is Darren going to leave his job?

No, he isn't.

b) Does Darren want to go around the world?

_____

c) Does Lucy like the garden?

_____

d) Is Darren's home big and new?

_____

e) Who is Darren going to give the money to?

_____

f) What is Darren going to buy?

_____

Presenter:	Congratulations, Darren Brown. You are the winner tonight on *Do YOU Want to be a Millionaire?* You win one million pounds. You're a very rich man! What are you going to do with the money, Darren?
Darren:	Er, oh, I don't know. It's a lot of money.
Presenter:	Are you going to leave your job?
Darren:	No. I love my job. I hope to do my job for many years until I retire.
Presenter:	What do you do, Darren?
Darren:	I'm a bus driver.
Presenter:	Well, what about travel? Do you want to go around the world?
Darren:	Why? No, I don't want to travel. Anyway, Lucy doesn't like travelling. She likes being at home in the garden.
Presenter:	So are you going to buy a big new house with a big garden for Lucy?
Darren:	No. I wouldn't like to move. Our house is very small, but Lucy and I like it. And it's near the park.
Presenter:	OK. What are you going to change in your life, then?
Darren:	Nothing. I'm very happy.
Presenter:	But what about the money? What are you going to do with all the money?
Darren:	I'm going to give it to the old dogs' home.
Presenter:	What will your wife Lucy think about that?
Darren:	Lucy? My wife? No, Lucy's my dog.
Presenter:	Er, right, I see.
Darren:	Actually, there is one thing I want to buy. I'm going to spend some of the money on a new bicycle.

Pronunciation

1 🌀 67 Listen to the sounds /ɒ/ and /əʊ/.

/ɒ/ l<u>o</u>ts　　/əʊ/ cl<u>o</u>thes

2 🌀 68 Listen to the words in the box. Is the <u>underlined</u> sound /ɒ/ or /əʊ/? Put the words in the correct column.

~~cl<u>o</u>thes~~　d<u>o</u>n't　h<u>o</u>me　h<u>o</u>pe　~~l<u>o</u>ts~~　opera
p<u>o</u>p　sh<u>o</u>w　s<u>o</u>ap　st<u>o</u>p　w<u>a</u>nt　w<u>a</u>tch

/ɒ/	/əʊ/
lots	clothes
_____	_____
_____	_____
_____	_____
_____	_____
_____	_____

🌀 69 Listen and check. Repeat the words.

Writing

Linking sentences: *and, but, because*
Completing a form, giving reasons

1 Read the advert and Angela's form. Why does Angela want to be on *Do YOU Want to be a Millionaire?* Tick (✓) three reasons.

a) She wants to be on TV. ☐

b) She wants to win money to go to university. ☐

c) She wants money to buy clothes. ☐

d) She wants money to pay off her debt and leave her job. ☐

> **Do you want to win a lot of money?**
> **Would you like to be on TV?**
>
> **If you answered *Yes* to these questions, go to our website and complete the form.**

Name Angela Ford

Telephone numbers
mobile 0798 78665
home 01765 55643
email address a.ford11@mailbox.com
job teacher

Tell us in about 100 words why you want to be on *Do YOU Want to be a Millionaire?*

I'm 25 and I'm a teacher in a secondary school. I work really hard, but I don't earn a lot. Also, I have a large debt from university. I would like to win a lot of money because I want to leave my job and pay off my debt. Also, I want more money because I really like clothes and shoes, but at the moment I don't have money to buy a lot of things.

I want to go on TV because I want to be famous. Millions of people watch *Do YOU Want to be a Millionaire?*

2 Complete the sentences about Angela using *and, but* and *because*.

a) Angela is poor _____ she doesn't earn a lot and she has a big debt.

b) Angela is a teacher _____ she works really hard.

c) Angela likes buying clothes _____ she has no money.

3 Complete the rules about *and, but* and *because*.

a) You use _____ to talk about the cause of a situation. It answers the question *Why?*

b) You use _____ to join two ideas.

c) You use _____ to contrast two different ideas.

4 Imagine you want to be on *Do YOU Want to be a Millionaire?* Complete the sentences.

a) I'm ... (describe yourself)

_____

_____

b) I would like to win a lot of money because ... (give three reasons)

_____

_____

c) I want to be on TV because ... (give a reason)

_____

_____

5 Complete the form for yourself. Use *and, but* and *because* and the sentences you wrote in Exercise 4 to help you.

Name

Telephone numbers
mobile
home
email address
job

Tell us in about 100 words why you want to be on *Do YOU Want to be a Millionaire?*

15 Experiences

Grammar

1 **Write the words in the correct order.**

a) to Australia been I've .

I've been to Australia.

b) Paris has to Clara been .

_____

c) been They haven't to Japan .

_____

d) been Dan over has 30 countries to .

_____

e) have My times been to six parents Spain .

_____

f) Berlin to haven't been I .

_____

g) twice We been to have Hong Kong .

_____

2 **Complete the sentences with the present perfect form of the verbs (in brackets).**

a) I ___'ve driven___ in the desert. (drive)

b) Lucy _____ with dolphins. (swim)

c) Mark _____ a Ferrari. (drive)

d) My sister and her husband _____ on a farm. (work)

e) I _____ the Queen. (meet)

f) My brother and I _____ across the Atlantic. (sail)

g) They _____ The Rolling Stones. (see)

3 **Underline the correct answer.**

a) I **have been** / went to Istanbul three times in my life.

b) Last year Betty **has been** / **went** to Madrid for the weekend.

c) My mother **has seen** / **saw** U2 six times. She's so lucky.

d) I **haven't been** / **didn't go** to New Zealand before. This is my first first time outside Europe.

e) In February Carlos **has met** / **met** an interesting woman in New York.

f) We **have bought** / **bought** a new car yesterday.

4 **Write questions with *Have you ever ... ?***

a) work / in a shop?

Have you ever worked in a shop?

b) see / someone famous?

_____

c) lose / something valuable?

_____

d) read / a book in one day?

_____

e) fly / in a small plane?

_____

5 **Write true short answers to the questions in Exercise 4. For *yes* answers give more information about when you had the experience.**

Example (a)

Yes, I have. In 1997 I worked in a record shop in Soho.

a) _____

_____

b) _____

_____

c) _____

_____

d) _____

_____

e) _____

_____

Vocabulary

1 Find the eight past participles in the wordsquare.

S	H	A	K	E	N	S	F	S	D
D	B	N	A	O	D	T	L	Y	H
O	D	E	S	I	A	E	O	A	A
N	E	N	A	G	F	S	W	U	M
E	D	R	I	V	E	N	N	O	A
W	O	N	D	D	T	I	R	I	S
I	N	M	W	O	R	K	E	D	D

a) shake   _shaken_

b) do   _____

c) drive   _____

d) fly   _____

e) say   _____

f) swim   _____

g) win   _____

h) work   _____

2 Complete the sentences with past participles of the verbs in the box.

break	buy	give	have	know
lose	~~meet~~	read	see	speak

a) I have never ___met___ anyone famous, but I have _____ to a famous actor on the phone.

b) Katy loves Leonardo DiCaprio. She's _____ all his films.

c) The most expensive thing he's ever _____ is his car. It was £30,000!

d) *War and Peace* is the longest book I've ever _____ .

e) Linda and Pat have _____ a few problems with their mother.

f) I have _____ Dan for twenty years. We were at school together.

g) My brother has _____ his leg six times.

h) I have never _____ my passport.

i) Tony has _____ me some great ideas for songs.

3 Complete the conversations with the words in the box. Then listen and check your answers.

bill	everything	have	like
menu	ready	Smoking	
something	~~table~~	Would	

Waiter: Good evening, sir, madam.

Man: Good evening. A (1) _table_ for two, please.

Waiter: (2) _____ or non-smoking?

Man: Non-smoking, please.

Waiter: Would you like (3) _____ to drink?

Woman: I'll (4) _____ a glass of water.

Man: And we'd like a bottle of champagne.

Waiter: Certainly.

Waiter: Are you (5) _____ to order?

Woman: Yes. I'd (6) _____ the chicken.

Man: And I'll have the salmon, please.

Waiter: (7) _____ you like to see the dessert (8) _____ ?

Woman: No, thank you.

Man: Yes, please.

Waiter: Was (9) _____ all right with your meal?

Man: Lovely, thank you.

Woman: Could we have the (10) _____ , please?

Waiter: Certainly.

70 Listen and check.

Reading

1 Read the travel forum. Tick (✓) the three photos of places or experiences the writers talk about.

Address: @ http://www.tf4u.com/forums/travel/3729.html   › go

Travel forum The place for people who love to travel

Joanna

Swimming with dolphins

Does anyone know where I can go to swim with dolphins? (I want to swim with wild dolphins, not in a swimming pool.) I would like to hear from people who have had the experience themselves. Thanks.   REPLY ○

Will
POSTED
29.05
9:20pm

RE: Swimming with dolphins

Swimming with dolphins in the sea should be a fantastic experience. I haven't done it but I've spoken to people who have done it. They all say Sinai is a good place, especially around Nuweiba. I recommend Sinai. I've been there many times. There is no better place to go than the Red Sea.   REPLY ○

AquaSue
POSTED
29.05
9:27pm

RE: Swimming with dolphins

I recommend Isla de Mujeres (it means 'island of women') in Mexico. The island is next to Cancun, which is a famous Mexican holiday destination. I've been to Isla de Mujeres three times and I've swum with dolphins twice. The dolphins swim freely in the sea and they're really friendly. It's a fantastic experience.   REPLY ○

Mary
POSTED
29.05
9:29pm

Holiday in the Alps

We're thinking about staying at the Hotel du Lac in Interlaken, Switzerland. Has anyone been there? It would be good to get some information.   REPLY ○

Klaus
POSTED
29.05
9:32pm

RE: Holiday in the Alps

We've been to Interlaken many times. We haven't stayed at the Hotel du Lac but it looks very nice. The name means 'hotel of the lake' but it's actually on a river between two lakes. Interlaken is a lovely place. There are a lot of tourists but I don't mind them. You can go up the Jungfrau mountain from Interlaken. It's a wonderful experience.   REPLY ○

Internet zone

a

b

c

d

2 <u>Underline</u> the correct answer.

a) Joanna had **one reply** / <u>**two replies**</u>.

b) Joanna wants to swim with dolphins in **the sea** / **a swimming pool**.

c) Isla de Mujeres means 'island of **men** / **women**'.

d) AquaSue **liked** / **didn't like** swimming with dolphins.

e) The Hotel du Lac is on a **lake** / **river**.

f) There **are** / **aren't** a lot of tourists in Interlaken.

3 Are the statements true (T) or false (F)?

a) Joanna has swum with dolphins. _F_

b) Will hasn't ever swum with dolphins.

_____

c) Will hasn't been to Sinai. _____

d) Will likes the Red Sea. _____

e) AquaSue has swum with dolphins three times. _____

f) Klaus has stayed at the Hotel du Lac many times. _____

g) Klaus hates the tourists in Interlaken.

_____

Writing

Forming and answering *Wh* questions
Building a text from notes

1 Read the travel forum and answer the questions.

a) What were Elaine's two questions?

i) _____

ii) _____

b) What was Dan's answer to the first question?

_____

c) What was TravelGirl's answer to the second question? _____

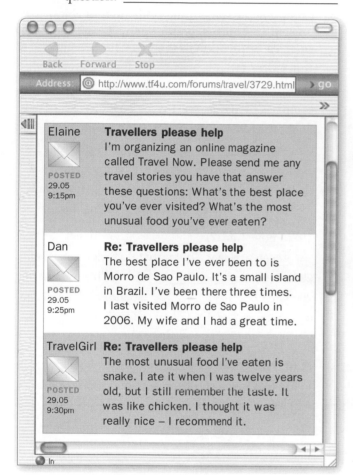

Address: @ http://www.tf4u.com/forums/travel/3729.html › go

Elaine **Travellers please help**
I'm organizing an online magazine called Travel Now. Please send me any travel stories you have that answer these questions: What's the best place you've ever visited? What's the most unusual food you've ever eaten?
POSTED 29.05 9:15pm

Dan **Re: Travellers please help**
The best place I've ever been to is Morro de Sao Paulo. It's a small island in Brazil. I've been there three times. I last visited Morro de Sao Paulo in 2006. My wife and I had a great time.
POSTED 29.05 9:25pm

TravelGirl **Re: Travellers please help**
The most unusual food I've eaten is snake. I ate it when I was twelve years old, but I still remember the taste. It was like chicken. I thought it was really nice – I recommend it.
POSTED 29.05 9:30pm

2 Complete the questions with the words in the box.

Where	What	How	Would	When

The best place you've visited

a) __What__ 's the name of the place? ☐

b) _____ is it? ☐

c) _____ many times have you been there? ☐

d) _____ did you last go there? ☐

e) _____ you recommend it? ☐

The most unusual food you've eaten

f) _____ many times have you eaten it? ☐

g) _____ did you first eat it? ☐

h) _____ did you think of it? ☐

i) _____ you recommend it? ☐

3 Tick (✓) the questions in Exercise 2 which were answered in the text in Exercise 1.

4 Think of the best place you've been to and the most unusual food you've eaten. Write answers to the questions in Exercise 2.

Example (a)

Barcelona _____

a) _____

b) _____

c) _____

d) _____

e) _____

f) _____

g) _____

h) _____

i) _____

5 Write a reply to Elaine in Exercise 1. Use your answers from Exercise 4.

Address: @ http://www.tf4u.com/forums/travel/3729.html › go

Name:
Re: Travellers please help

Pronunciation

1 Circle the past participle in each group that has a different vowel sound from the others.

a) w<u>o</u>n d<u>o</u>ne (g<u>o</u>ne) r<u>u</u>n

b) h<u>ur</u>t c<u>au</u>ght b<u>ou</u>ght t<u>au</u>ght

c) pl<u>ay</u>ed m<u>a</u>de p<u>ai</u>d s<u>ai</u>d

d) sl<u>e</u>pt b<u>ee</u>n m<u>e</u>t m<u>ea</u>nt

🔊 **71** Listen and check.

2 Put the past participles from the box into the correct group in Exercise 1.

r<u>ea</u>d	sh<u>a</u>ken	sw<u>u</u>m	th<u>ou</u>ght

🔊 **72** Listen and check.

16 Drive

Grammar

1 Complete the questions with the words in the box.

> about   for   ~~from~~   to   to   with

a) Where do you come ___*from*___ ?

b) When you're with your friends, what do you talk _____ ?

c) What kind of music do you listen _____ ?

d) Who do you usually go on holiday _____ ?

e) How many countries have you been _____ ?

f) Which company would you like to work _____ ?

2 Write true answers to the questions in Exercise 1.

Example (a)

> *I come from Poland.*

a) _____

b) _____

c) _____

d) _____

e) _____

f) _____

3 Complete the sentences. Use the present simple or present continuous form of the verb in brackets.

a) I _____*have*_____ breakfast at eight o'clock every morning. (have)

b) Come on! Dave _____ for us. (wait)

c) I _____ football or basketball. (not like)

d) No, I can't come out now. I _____ a really good film. (watch)

e) Hello? Sorry, I can't talk at the moment – I _____ . (drive)

f) It usually _____ me an hour to get to work. (take)

4 <u>Underline</u> the correct form of the verb.

a) I **went** / **'ve been** to 36 countries in my life.

b) **Did you have** / **Have you had** a good time last night?

c) Could you choose another DVD? I **saw** / **'ve seen** this one.

d) I **went** / **'ve been** to see The White Stripes last year.

e) John Lennon (1940–1980) **wrote** / **has written** more than 200 songs.

f) Brazil **won** / **have won** the football World Cup five times.

5 Complete the story. Choose the present simple, present continuous, present perfect, past simple or *going to* future form of the verbs (in brackets).

Tom Curtis (1) _____*is*_____ (be) a travel fanatic. He (2) _____ (go) to ninety-four countries in his life. Next week he (3) _____ (visit) the ninety-fifth, Nigeria. But Tom never (4) _____ (fly) to the places he visits, he always (5) _____ (travel) by motorbike. At the moment, he (6) _____ (get) ready for his long journey from London to Nigeria.

Up to now Tom (7) _____ (have) seventeen accidents, but only two serious ones. In 2001, he (8) _____ (break) his leg and in 2005 he (9) _____ (spend) two months in a hospital in Kazakhstan after a bad fall.

Tom (10) _____ (start) his journey in four days' time. He (11) _____ (want) to get to Nigeria and back in two months. Good luck, Tom!

🌐 73 **Listen and check.**

Vocabulary

1 Look at the pictures and complete the crossword.

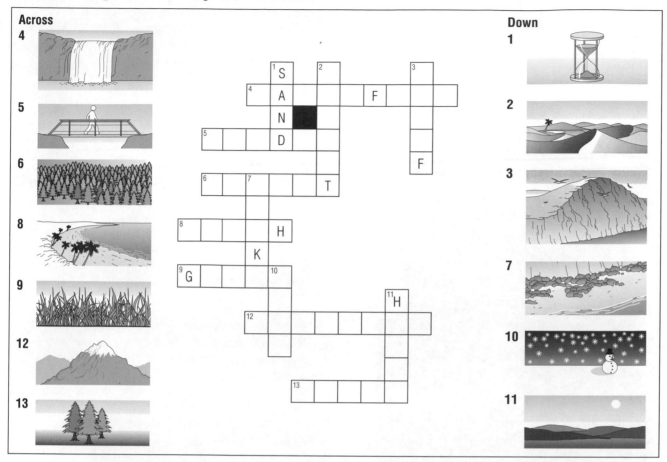

2 Complete the sentences with the words in the box.

across	along	~~down~~	into	out of
over	past	through	up	

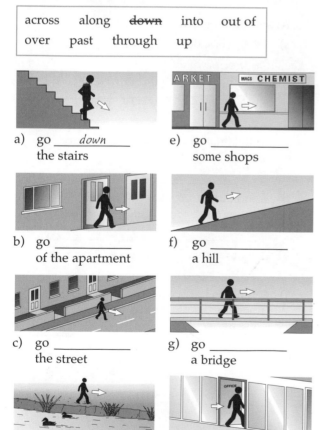

a) go _____down_____ the stairs

b) go _____ of the apartment

c) go _____ the street

d) go _____ the river

e) go _____ some shops

f) go _____ a hill

g) go _____ a bridge

h) go _____ my office

3 Complete the conversation with the words in the box.

~~down~~	end	on	opposite
straight	turn	turning	

Dave: Hi, Angie. I'm on the High Street. How do I get to your place?

Angie: Great. Go (1) _____down_____ the High Street and take the second (2) _____ on the right.

Dave: Is that Ash Road?

Angie: Yes. That was fast!

Dave: I'm on my bike.

Angie: OK, go to the (3) _____ of Ash Road and (4) _____ left into Beech Road.

Dave: OK.

Angie: Then go (5) _____ on and there's a pub (6) _____ the right. Our house is (7) _____ the pub. Number 24.

Dave: Great! See you in a minute.

🔘 74 **Listen and check.**

Listening

1 🔘 **75 Cover the listening script. Listen to three people talking about beautiful drives. Match each drive to a photo.**

a) Highway 1:   photo _____

b) Picos de Europa: photo _____

c) Route 62:   photo _____

2 Listen again. Which drive are these statements about? Write *H* (Highway 1) , *P* (Picos de Europa), or *R* (Route 62).

a) The drive takes three days. _*H*_

b) It goes through a National Park. _____

c) It goes through a wine-making region. _____

d) It's a good place for people who like walking. _____

e) You see wonderful views of the sea. _____

f) It goes along a river. _____

Highway 1 in the USA is a wonderful drive. It goes along the Pacific coast from Los Angeles to San Francisco. The scenery is spectacular. The road goes along the cliffs, so there are fantastic views of the ocean. I went with my boyfriend, Richard. We drove a 1962 Corvette and the journey took three days. In San Francisco we drove over the Golden Gate Bridge. I'll never forget it! On Highway 1 drive slowly so you can enjoy the views and don't drive off the cliffs!

The Picos de Europa is a range of mountains on the north coast of Spain. It was Spain's first National Park. The road through this beautiful region is probably the best drive in Europe. I did this trip with my family last summer. We started in Santander and drove over the mountains and through green valleys, where we saw horses in the fields. This is a great place for walking. The Picos de Europa Park is very beautiful, but quite small. A lot of tourists go there in the summer, so it's best to go in spring.

Route 62 in South Africa is an old road that goes between Cape Town and Oudtshoorn. It's one of the most beautiful roads in the country, and follows the Breede river through a green valley with trees and wild flowers. This area is also famous for its wine-making and there are lots of interesting places where you can stop and eat. The N2 – 'the Garden Route' – is near Route 62. It's probably South Africa's most famous road, but there's a lot of traffic on it. I think Route 62 is quieter and more interesting than N2.

3 Answer the questions.

a) What coast does Highway 1 go along?

the Pacific coast

b) How long does it take to drive from San Francisco to Los Angeles?

_____

c) What animals do you see in the Picos de Europa?

_____

d) Who did the speaker travel with in the Picos de Europa?

_____

e) What famous road is Route 62 near?

_____

f) What kind of scenery does Route 62 go through?

_____

Writing

Using adjectives to make a text more interesting
Describing a journey

1 Read the notes about a journey and complete the text.

An amazing journey

WHERE	London to Scotland
WHO WITH	My best friend, Bonnie
CAR	Bonnie's Ford Escort
TRAFFIC	Busy until Scotland, then quieter
SCENERY	Mountains, rivers, lakes
HOW FAR	600 miles
HOW LONG	3 days

Last summer I did an amazing journey from my home in (1) _London_ to the north of Scotland. I went with my best friend, Bonnie, in her old Ford Escort. From London to Carlisle, the traffic was terrible, and the roads were very (2) _____ . But in Scotland the roads were much (3) _____ and the scenery was spectacular. The road goes through beautiful (4) _____ , along rivers and by (5) _____ , and we saw lots of wild animals and birds. The views were fantastic! We travelled (6) _____ miles in (7) _____ days.

2 Adjectives make a text more interesting. Read the text again, and write the adjectives the writer uses to describe these things.

a) the journey _____amazing_____

b) the Ford Escort _____

c) the traffic _____

d) the scenery _____

e) the mountains _____

f) the views _____

3 Think of a journey you have made. Make notes about it.

An amazing journey

WHERE	_____
WHO WITH	_____
CAR	_____
TRAFFIC	_____
SCENERY	_____
HOW FAR	_____
HOW LONG	_____

4 Write about your journey. Use the notes you made in Exercise 3. Use adjectives to make your text more interesting.

Pronunciation

🔊 **76** Listen to the sentences and <u>underline</u> the stressed words.

a) The <u>mountains</u> were <u>spectacular</u>.

b) The traffic is terrible.

c) My car is so old.

d) What beautiful shoes!

e) This weather is fantastic.

f) The views were amazing.

Practise saying the sentences.

Story: *The Canterville Ghost*

by Stephen Colbourn

Mr Hiram B. Otis was a rich American from New York. He had come to live and work in England, but he did not want to live in London. He did not want to live in the city. He wanted to live in the countryside outside London.

Canterville Chase was a large and very old house near London. Lord Canterville, the owner, wanted to sell it. So Mr Hiram B. Otis visited Lord Canterville.

'I do not live in Canterville Chase,' Lord Canterville said to Mr Otis. 'I do not want to live there. The house has a ghost – The Canterville Ghost.'

'I come from America,' said Mr Otis. 'America is a modern country. I don't believe in ghosts. Have you seen this Canterville Ghost?'

'No,' said Lord Canterville, 'but I have heard it at night.'

'I don't believe in ghosts,' Mr Otis said again. 'No one has found a ghost. No one has put a ghost in a museum. And you haven't seen this ghost either.'

'But several members of my family have seen it,' said Lord Canterville. 'My aunt saw the ghost. She was so frightened that she was ill for the rest of her life. Also, the servants have seen it so they will not stay in the house at night. Only the housekeeper, Mrs Umney, lives in Canterville Chase. Mrs Umney lives there alone.'

'I want to buy the house,' said Mr Otis. 'I'll buy the ghost as well. Will you sell Canterville Chase? Will you sell the ghost?'

'Yes, I will,' said Lord Canterville. 'But, please remember, I told you about the ghost before you bought the house.'

Mr Hiram B. Otis bought Canterville Chase. Then his family came to England from America. He had a wife called Lucretia, three sons and a daughter.

The eldest son, Washington, was almost twenty years old. He was good-looking and had fair hair. His two young brothers were twins. They were twelve years old. The daughter, Virginia, was fifteen years old. She had large blue eyes and a lovely face.

Mr Otis took his family to live at Canterville Chase. The old house was in the countryside west of London. Mr Otis and his family travelled from London by train. Then they rode to the house in a wagon pulled by two horses.

Canterville Chase was big and old. Trees grew all around the house. The Otis family wanted to stop and look at the outside of the house, but the sky darkened. A thunderstorm was coming. Rain started to fall, so the family went inside the house quickly.

Mrs Umney, the housekeeper, was waiting for them by the front door. She was an old woman and wore a black dress and white apron. She lived at Canterville Chase and looked after the house.

'Welcome to Canterville Chase,' said Mrs Umney. 'Would you like some tea?'

'Yes, please,' said Mrs Otis.

The Otis family followed Mrs Umney into the library. There was a big table in the centre of the room and many chairs. Mrs Umney put teacups on the table, then she brought a pot of tea.

The Otises sat in the library and drank their tea. They looked out of a large window at the rain. The rain was falling heavily and the sky was black. They heard thunder and they saw lightning.

Mrs Otis looked around the room. There were many books on bookshelves. There were paintings on the walls. There was also a red stain on the floor. The red stain was by the fireplace.

'What is this red stain?' Mrs Otis asked Mrs Umney.

'It is blood,' answered the old housekeeper in a quiet voice.

'I don't want a blood-stain in my library,' said Mrs Otis. 'Please remove the stain. Please clean the floor immediately.'

The old woman smiled. 'It is the blood of Lady Eleanore de Canterville. She was murdered by her husband, Sir Simon de Canterville, in 1575. The blood-stain has been here for over three hundred years. It cannot be removed.'

'Nonsense,' said Washington Otis. 'I have some Pinkerton's Stain Remover from America. It can remove any stain. Watch.'

Washington Otis took the stain remover from a bag. Pinkerton's Stain Remover looked like a small black stick. He rubbed the stick on the blood-stain. A minute later the floor was clean. The stick had removed the stain quickly and easily.

Mrs Umney looked at the floor. She was frightened. No one had removed the blood-stain for three hundred years. Mrs Umney was very frightened.

'Pinkerton's can remove anything,' said Washington Otis. 'The blood-stain has gone.'

Lightning flashed and lit the library. Thunder crashed over the house. Mrs Umney fainted.

Mr and Mrs Otis ran across the library. They helped the old housekeeper who lay on the floor. Mrs Umney's eyes were closed and her face was pale.

'Mrs Umney! Mrs Umney!' cried Mrs Otis. 'Can you speak?'

Mrs Umney opened her eyes. 'Trouble will come to this house,' she said. 'I have seen the ghost. The ghost will come to you.'

Washington Otis rubbed Pinkerton's Stain Remover on the blood-stain.

All the Otises helped Mrs Umney to stand up. 'The ghost will come,' she said again. 'You must not remove the blood-stain. You must not clean the library floor. The ghost will be angry.'

Then Mrs Umney went upstairs to her room.

'Let's look for the ghost,' said the Otis boys. 'Let's look round the house.'

The Otises looked round the house together. But they did not see the Canterville Ghost.

That night the family went to bed early. The storm continued all night. Next morning they went into the library. The blood-stain had reappeared on the floor.

'I'll remove this blood-stain once more,' said Washington Otis. 'Mother doesn't want a blood-stain in the library. I'll clean the floor again.'

He removed the blood-stain with Pinkerton's Stain Remover. The library floor was clean. But the next morning the stain had come back again.

'This is very strange,' said Mr Otis. 'I'll lock the library door at night. No one can come into the library. No one can put a stain on the floor.'

'I don't think Pinkerton's Stain Remover is bad,' said Washington Otis. 'I think there really is a ghost. The ghost is making the blood-stain. The ghost puts the stain on the floor at night.'

'We must find this ghost,' said Mr Hiram B. Otis. 'It must stop making these stains. Your mother does not like blood on the library floor.'

That day the family went out. They walked around the countryside near Canterville Chase. They went to the nearby village. They looked at the old village houses. Then they walked back to Canterville Chase through the woods. It was a summer evening and the weather was fine.

It was late when they got back to the house. The Otises were hungry and tired. After eating supper they went to bed. The bedrooms were upstairs. There was a long corridor upstairs. The bedroom doors were along this corridor.

Mr Otis woke up after midnight. There was a strange noise outside his room. The sound was like metal chains. The chains were rubbing together.

Mr Otis got out of bed and opened the bedroom door. He looked into the corridor.

He saw the Canterville Ghost in the corridor. The ghost was an old man with burning red eyes. He had long grey hair and wore very old-fashioned clothes. There were chains on his hands and feet. He was rubbing the chains together so they made a noise.

'My dear sir, your chains make a terrible noise,' Mr Otis said to the ghost. 'You must put some oil on those chains. Here is some Tammany Rising Sun Oil from the United States. Please put the oil on your chains.'

Mr Otis put a bottle of oil on a table in the corridor. Then he closed his bedroom door and went back to bed.

The Canterville Ghost was very surprised. He had lived in Canterville Chase for three hundred years. Everyone was frightened of him, because everyone was afraid of ghosts. But this American gentleman was not afraid.

The Canterville Ghost decided to work harder. He wanted to frighten the American. He made a terrible noise and shone a horrible green light in the corridor.

Another door opened at the end of the corridor. Mr Otis's youngest sons came out of their bedroom. The two young boys had the pillows from their beds in their hands. They threw the pillows at the ghost. They laughed at the ghost.

'Here is some Tammany Rising Sun Oil,' said Mr Otis. 'Please put the oil on your chains.'

The ghost was amazed and upset. No one had laughed at him before. He was a ghost. Everyone is frightened of ghosts. No one had ever laughed at the Canterville Ghost before.

The Canterville Ghost did not know what to do. He disappeared through the wall and the house became quiet.

The ghost went to the secret room where he lived. He sat down on a chair. He thought about what had happened.

He had frightened people for three hundred years. He had looked through windows and frightened the servants. He had knocked on bedroom doors. He had frightened people in their beds. He had blown out candles in the night. He had turned green and made noises with his chains. Everyone had always been frightened. No one had given him Rising Sun Oil to put on his chains. No one had thrown pillows at him. He was a very unhappy ghost.

———————

Washington Otis removed the blood-stain in the library every day. Every morning the stain had reappeared. But the stain was no longer the colour of blood. One morning it was brown. Another morning it was purple. Then it became bright green.

The Otises laughed at the blood-stain. They looked for it every morning before breakfast.

'What colour is it today?' asked Washington Otis.

'It's green!' shouted the twins. 'It's green blood today.'

They laughed at the green blood-stain on the library floor.

Virginia Otis did not laugh. The young girl was silent at breakfast. The blood-stain made her feel sad and she almost cried when she saw the bright green stain. She was sure that the ghost put the stain on the floor. She felt sorry for the ghost.

'The stain has been here for three hundred years,' said Virginia. 'We have been here for three weeks. The poor ghost puts the stain on the floor every night. Can't you leave the stain there?'

But the others did not listen to Virginia.

———————

The second appearance of the ghost was on a Sunday night. The Otises had all gone to bed. Suddenly they were woken up. They heard a terrible crashing noise downstairs.

The whole family ran out of their bedrooms. They ran downstairs. It was dark but Mr Otis and his eldest son carried candles. They heard another crashing noise in the hallway near the front door.

There was a suit of armour in the hallway. This suit of armour was more than three hundred years old. It had fallen over and made a loud noise. The Canterville Ghost was sitting on the floor next to the armour.

The ghost had tried to put on the suit of armour. He wanted to walk around the house and frighten the Otis family. But the metal suit was too heavy. The suit of armour had fallen onto the floor.

The Canterville Ghost was sitting beside the armour. He was rubbing his knee. He had hurt himself.

Mr Hiram B. Otis pointed a gun at the ghost. Washington Otis held his candle high in the air. The Otis twins laughed loudly. Virginia was afraid and stood beside her mother. They all looked at the Canterville Ghost.

The ghost was very angry. He stood up and gave a loud shout. He blew out the candle in Washington Otis's hand. There was no light in the hall. Then the ghost ran up the stairs in the darkness.

He stopped at the top of the stairs and laughed. He had a frightening laugh. Men's hair had turned grey when they heard him laugh. But the Otises were not afraid.

'Are you in pain?' asked Mrs Otis. 'I have a bottle of Dr Dobell's medicine. It is good for stomach-aches and headaches. Please take the medicine.'

The ghost looked at Mrs Otis angrily. Then he disappeared in a green cloud and went back to his secret room. He was very unhappy. He had tried to put on the suit of armour, but it was too heavy. The armour had fallen over and the ghost had hurt his leg.

———————

The ghost stayed in his room during the day. He came out at night to visit the library. He repainted the blood-stain every night. And every morning, Washington Otis removed the blood-stain with Pinkerton's Stain Remover.

But the ghost had a problem. He had quickly finished all his red paint. Now his brown and purple paints were finished as well. So, sometimes he painted the blood-stain green, sometimes blue.

The ghost made plans. He wanted to frighten the Otis twins. He planned to visit the twins in the night. He planned to turn himself green and make a horrible noise. He planned to visit the twins in their bedroom. He planned to touch them with his ice-cold hands in the dark.

He left his secret room at midnight. The house was dark. He climbed the stairs and walked along the corridor. The twins' bedroom was at the end of the corridor round a corner. He turned the corner. Suddenly he stopped.

In front of him was a round face with a terrible mouth and burning eyes. Fire shone out of the mouth and eyes of this horrible face. It was the face of a ghost!

The Canterville Ghost gave a shout and ran back to his secret room. He had never seen a ghost before and felt very frightened.

Before daylight came, the Canterville Ghost felt better. Were there two ghosts in the house? He must find out. He must meet the second ghost.

He went back upstairs and walked along the corridor towards the twins' room. The second ghost was still there, but its eyes were no longer burning. He went up to it. He touched it. The head of the second ghost fell onto the floor. It was not a ghost at all. It was a head made from a large round vegetable called a pumpkin. The twins had put a candle inside it. There was a card on the floor.

THE OTIS GHOST
THE ONLY TRUE
CANTERVILLE GHOST

The twins had put the head in the corridor to frighten him. This made the Canterville Ghost very angry. What could he do? He could think of nothing at that moment, so he went back to his room.

The ghost felt very weak and tired. He stayed in his room for five days. He did not repaint the blood-stain in the library. There had been a blood-stain on the library floor for three hundred years. Now the library floor was clean.

After a week the ghost felt better. He decided to try once more to frighten the Otis twins. He planned to make his face look as horrible as possible. He waited until the middle of the night.

Slowly and silently he walked to the twins' bedroom. It was one o'clock in the morning. The house was quiet. The door of the twins' room was slightly open.

The ghost took off his head and carried it under his arm. It is terrifying to see a headless ghost. He wanted to terrify the twins.

He pushed open the door of the twins' bedroom. The door banged against the wall.

He had planned to shout and hold his head in his hands. But a heavy jug of water fell from the top of the door. The twins had played a trick on him. He was soaked with water. The twins shouted and laughed.

The ghost ran back down the corridor. He could not frighten the twins. He could not frighten anyone in the Otis family.

Washington Otis came out of his bedroom. The ghost stopped running. Behind him, the twins ran down the corridor. They shouted – 'Boo!' – in his ears and waved their arms. Washington Otis laughed at him.

The ghost did not know what to do. He ran through the nearest door, went back to the secret room and lay down. He could not frighten anyone. He was a very unhappy ghost.

The Otises did not see the Canterville ghost at night again. The twins waited for him when it was dark. They put a rope across the corridor. They tied metal tins to the rope. But the ghost did not walk into the tins. Only Mr Otis came along the corridor. He fell over the rope and was very angry.

Virginia Otis was also angry with the twins. 'Can't you leave the poor ghost alone?' she said. 'Why do you want to hurt him? Why do you want to play tricks on him? He has lived here for a very long time. Leave him alone.'

The twins did not listen, but the ghost heard Virginia's words. The words gave him hope.

One afternoon, Virginia went to the library. The library door was slightly open. She pushed the door wide open and quietly walked into the room.

There was somebody sitting by the window. It was the Canterville Ghost!

He was looking at the library window which was made of coloured glass. There were words painted on the glass.

He was wearing his best clothes and had combed his long grey hair.

'I feel very sorry for you,' said Virginia quietly. 'I'm sorry that my brothers were not very kind to you. But you did try to frighten them.'

'Yes, I did,' said the ghost. 'It is my job to frighten everyone who comes to Canterville Chase.'

'You are very wicked, I know,' said Virginia. 'Mrs Umney, the housekeeper, told us that you killed your wife.'

'Yes, I did,' replied the ghost. 'But she wasn't very kind. And it wasn't very kind of her brothers to starve me to death.'

'Starve you to death?' said Virginia. 'Oh, poor ghost, are you hungry? Would you like a sandwich?'

'No, thank you,' he replied. 'I never eat anything. But you are very kind. You are much kinder than the rest of your family. They are rude, nasty and unkind.'

'Stop!' cried Virginia. 'You are nasty and unkind too. You stole my paint box. You used my paints to make the blood-stain in the library. I never told anyone about it. But now I'm going to fetch my father.'

She turned to go, but the ghost spoke again.

'Please do not go, Miss Virginia,' said the ghost. 'I am so lonely and so unhappy. I do not know what to do. I want to go to sleep and I cannot.'

'It's easy to sleep,' said Virginia. 'You go to bed and close your eyes.'

'I have not slept for three hundred years,' said the ghost. 'I have not slept since I was murdered by my wife's brothers.'

Virginia walked across the library and looked at the old face of the ghost. It was a sad face.

'Poor ghost,' said Virginia, 'how can I help you to sleep?'

'Far away in the woods,' said the ghost, 'there is a little garden. In the little garden the grass grows long and thick. There are many flowers and trees. A nightingale sings all night long. The bird's sweet song is beautiful and sad. The white stars and the pale moon look down on this little garden. It is very peaceful.'

Virginia's eyes were full of tears. She put her hands over her face.

'You mean it is the Garden of Death,' she said quietly.

'Yes, the Garden of Sleep,' said the ghost. 'It is very beautiful. There is peace and silence. There is no yesterday

'Look,' said the ghost. 'Read the lines on the window.'

The Canterville Ghost

and no tomorrow. But only Love can open the door to the garden. For Love is stronger than Death.'

Virginia did not know what to say. She listened as the ghost spoke again.

'Have you read the writing on the library window?'

'Yes,' said Virginia, 'but I do not understand it.'

'Look,' said the ghost. 'Read the lines on the window.'

Virginia looked at the window and read the lines of poetry:

When a golden girl shall weep
For the ghost that cannot sleep,
Then the dead at last shall die
And in restful earth may lie.

'The words mean you must weep for me,' said the unhappy ghost. 'Then the Angel of Death will let me rest. Will you help?'

'What do I have to do?' asked Virginia.

'You must come with me into the darkness. You will see strange things. You will hear strange voices, but nothing will hurt you. You are good and kind. The dark cannot hurt you.'

Virginia did not answer and the ghost waited. He had waited for three hundred years. This was the longest minute of all that time.

'I am not afraid,' said Virginia at last. 'I will come with you into the dark.'

The ghost kissed her hand. His lips were cold like ice, but they burned like fire. The ghost held her hand and they walked to the wall of the library. The wall opened. There was darkness beyond the wall and a cold wind. Voices spoke out of the wind. 'Go back, Virginia. Go back before it is too late.'

Virginia walked into the darkness with the ghost. Virginia and the ghost disappeared through the library wall.

———

Virginia did not come downstairs for supper. Mr Otis sent one of the servants to her room. The servant could not find Virginia so everybody searched the house. They looked everywhere but they could not find her. Mr and Mrs Otis were very worried.

It was a summer evening and the sun had not set, so the family and the servants searched the gardens before it was dark. In the garden there were many trees and a deep pond. They looked in the pond. They looked in the trees. Then they asked people at the railway station. But no one had seen Virginia. Mr Otis went to tell the village policeman that Virginia had disappeared. But, by that time, it was dark and no one could search any more that night.

None of the family wanted to eat or sleep. They sat in the library and waited. They hoped Virginia would return safely. They planned to search for Virginia again in the morning.

It was midnight when the family decided to go to bed. They left the library and started to walk up the stairs together. Suddenly all the clocks in the house struck twelve and they heard a terrible noise. Thunder crashed outside the house and the Otises heard a dreadful cry. Strange music sounded inside the house and a door opened at the top of the stairs.

Virginia stood in the doorway. She looked down the stairs at them. Her face was very pale and she carried a small box in her hand.

'Where have you been?' Mr Otis asked angrily. 'Your mother has been very worried. You have frightened us all. You must never play a trick like this again.'

'Except on the ghost,' said the twins. 'You can play tricks on the ghost!'

'Father,' Virginia said quietly, 'I have been with the ghost. He is dead and now he can rest. He gave me this box of beautiful jewels before he died.'

She showed her father the small box. Inside was a necklace made of red stones.

'Where did you get this?' asked her father. 'Where have you been?'

Mr Otis forgot to be angry. He was so pleased to see that Virginia was safe.

'Come. I'll show you,' said Virginia.

She turned back to the door at the top of the stairs. All of the family followed her. Washington Otis carried a lighted candle.

Virginia led them along a secret corridor. They came to an old wooden door which was open. Beyond the door was a little room with a low ceiling. There was an iron ring in the wall and two chains. At the end of the chains was a body. Only bones remained. It was a skeleton.

'This is the body of Sir Simon de Canterville,' said Virginia. 'He murdered his wife in 1575. Then his wife's brothers shut him in this room. He was given no food. Sir Simon starved to death. His ghost was in this house for three hundred years. But now he has found peace.'

The Otis family looked around the little room and did not know what to say. Virginia knelt on the floor beside the skeleton and began to pray.

There was a funeral four nights later. The Otises buried the body of Sir Simon de Canterville in a grave among the trees.

The Otises, Mrs Umney the housekeeper, and all the servants from Canterville Chase stood near the grave. Behind them were people from the nearby village. Many people had come to the funeral.

Virginia carried white flowers. She looked up at the stars and the pale moon and the dark trees. She remembered what the ghost had said about the Garden of Death. A nightingale began to sing. The bird's sweet song was beautiful and sad.

Virginia smiled. 'God has forgiven him for murdering his wife,' she said.

Answer key

1 Airport

Grammar

1
a) 'm; 's; 'm   b) 's; 's
c) Are; aren't
d) Is; 's   e) Are; 're

2
b) a   c) an   d) a   e) an   f) a

3
c) 's this; It's   d) are these; They're
e) 's this; It's   f) are these; They're
g) are these; They're

4
a) What's your phone number?
b) Are you British?
c) What's your email address?
d) What's in your bag?

Vocabulary

1

Country	Language
China	Chinese
Spain	Spanish
Italy	Italian
Poland	Polish
Japan	Japanese
Russia	Russian
Germany	German

2
2 two   3 three   4 four   5 five
6 six   7 seven   8 eight   9 nine
10 ten

3
a) aspirins   b) diary
c) mobile phone   d) sweets
e) umbrella   f) magazine
g) toothbrush   h) tissues
i) book   j) camera   k) watch
l) coin

4
2 do   3 repeat   4 Thanks

Listening

1
The order is: c), b), d), a).

2
b) 0703 5268 401   c) Joaquin
d) Spain   e) book   f) isn't
g) 603 380230

Pronunciation

2
1 VIP (Very Important Person)
2 USA (United States of America)
3 BBC (British Broadcasting Corporation)
4 FBI (Federal Bureau of Investigation)
5 UFO (Unidentified Flying Object)
6 CNN (Cable News Network)
7 UK (United Kingdom)
8 CIA (Central Intelligence Agency)

Writing

1 Rules a, b, c, d, e, f and h are correct.

2
b) I'm from Poland.
c) I live in New York.
d) My address is 42 Madison Avenue.
e) My home phone number is 001 212 299 001.
f) My email address is katrinab@info.com.

2 People

Grammar

1
b) your   c) her   d) His   e) Its
f) our   g) Their

2
b) He's my favourite actor.
c) Is her name Carla?
d) Joe is with his friend.
e) Our teacher is from New York.
f) Their grandparents are Arthur and Joan.

3

	Affirmative	Negative
I	'm	'm not
you	're	aren't
he/she/it	's	isn't
we	're	aren't
they	're	aren't

4
b) 's   c) 's   d) 's   e) are
f) are

5
b) My mother isn't a teacher.
c) My hairdresser isn't a man.
d) My favourite drink isn't tea.
e) My friends and I aren't students.
f) My grandparents aren't doctors.

6
b) Is your mother over 50 years old?
c) Is your teacher British?
d) Is your phone number 01807 322 486?
e) Are your classmates from Spain?
f) Are you and your family from Russia?

7
b) Yes, she is. / No, she isn't.
c) Yes, he/she is. / No, he/she isn't.
d) Yes, it is. / No, it isn't.
e) Yes, they are./ No, they aren't.
f) Yes, we are. / No, we aren't.

Vocabulary

1
b) food   c) sport   d) animal
e) drink   f) writer   g) film
h) singer

3
b) twenty-one
c) forty-six
d) seventy-three
e) a/one hundred and fifteen
f) three hundred and twelve

4
b) 45 x 10 = 450
c) 29 – 19 = 10
d) 113 + 76 = 189
e) 345 x 2 = 690
f) 460 + 279 = 739

5
1 lawyer
2 taxi driver
3 IT technician
4 shop assistant
5 hairdresser
6 sales manager
7 nurse
8 doctor

6
1 morning   2 How   3 well
4 you   5 bad   6 this   7 meet
8 Nice   9 See   10 Goodbye

Reading

1
a) Photo 2   b) Photo 1   c) Photo 3

2

b) Bill   c) Aleksy   d) Elena
e) Bill   f) Aleksy

3

b) 22   c) Yes   d) Spain
e) No, he's Polish.
f) No, she's a lawyer.

Writing

1

2 from   3 nurse   4 number
5 are   6 drink   7 singer

2 a) 2   b) 4   c) 1   d) 3

Pronunciation

1

b) 1 (cat)   c) 2 (wri – ter)
d) 1 (drink)   e) 2 (sing – er)
f) 3 (hair – dress – er)
g) 3 (e – le – ven)   h) 1 (food)
i) 1 (nurse)   j) 3 (an – i – mal)

3

b) <u>cat</u>   c) w<u>ri</u>ter   d) <u>drink</u>
e) <u>sing</u>er   f) <u>hair</u>dresser   g) <u>e</u>leven
h) <u>food</u>   i) <u>nurse</u>   j) <u>an</u>imal

3 Family

Grammar

1

b) sister's   c) brothers
d) children's

2

b) My sister's children are two and
   five.
c) My mother's name is Jane.
d) My brothers' names are Kelvin
   and Stan.
e) Paula's husband's name is Jerry.
f) Their children's names are Ben
   and Stevie.

3

b) does   c) has   d) is
e) watches   f) lives   g) works
h) buys

4

b) Johan has a big car.
c) You like computer games.
d) I live in Madrid.
e) The cat lives in my apartment.
f) They play football in the park.
g) My sister goes to bed late Fridays.
h) I do the housework in our house.
i) We eat our meals in the kitchen.
j) He watches TV in the evening.

6

2 is   3 works   4 does   5 buys
6 play   7 have   8 lives   9 goes
10 lives

Vocabulary

1

♂	♀
husband	wife
brother	sister
son	daughter
grandson	granddaughter
father	mother
uncle	aunt
cousin	cousin
nephew	niece
brother-in-law	sister-in-law
grandfather	grandmother

2

b) husband   c) sister   d) son
e) uncle   f) grandmother
g) granddaughter   h) mother
i) niece   j) nephew

4

2 Drive   3 worry   4 time
5 care   6 Call   7 forget

Listening

1

Brother and sister:
Andrea + Charlotte,
Charlotte + Pierre, Pauline + Louis
Cousins:
Andrea – Pauline, Louis – Charlotte

2

b) brother   c) Charlotte
d) skiing   e) Albert   f) Stephanie
g) cousin

3

b) F   c) T   d) T   e) F   f) T

Writing

1   a) and c) are correct

2

Michael's children's names are Dylan
and Carys. Michael's American. He's
married to Catherine. She's from
Wales. Her parents' names are Dai
and Pat, and Michael's parents'
names are Kirk and Diana. Dylan and
Carys have cousins in Britain and
America.

Pronunciation

2

a) brother and mother
b) buy and try
c) drink and think
d) eight and late
e) game and name
f) know and so
g) make and steak
h) Mr and sister
i) play and stay

4 Different

Grammar

1

b) I like football.
c) My father works in a bank.
d) My friends play football every
   weekend.
e) My aunt lives in Tokyo.
f) We go on holiday every year.

2

b) Does your father drink beer?
c) Do you like hip-hop?
d) Does your mother play tennis?
e) Do you do the housework?
f) Does your friend sing in a band?

4

b) doesn't like   c) doesn't play
d) don't work   e) doesn't sing
f) doesn't drink

5

2 him   3 them   4 her
5 us   6 you   7 it

Vocabulary

1

b) driving   f) cooking
c) dancing   g) reading
d) studying   h) shopping
e) jogging

2

b) I don't like it.   c) I really like it.
d) I like it.   e) I love it.   f) I hate it.

3

b) I don't like studying.
c) I hate cooking.
d) I don't mind driving.
e) I really like shopping.
f) I like dancing.

5

2 think   3 think   4 about
5 think   6 what   7 think
8 What   9 about   10 think

Reading

1 c)

2

b) T   c) F   d) F   e) T   f) F

3

a) 18
b) No, he lives with his parents and
   two sisters.
c) football and swimming
d) Yes, she loves it.
e) No, she doesn't.
f) She goes out.

Writing

1   b) 1   c) 5   d) 2   e) 3

2

Hi

My name's is John. I'm 32 and I'm from England. I live in Leeds and I'm a sales manager. I have three brothers and two sisters. My mum's a doctor and my dad's a bus driver.

What about you? Do you have a large family?

I like swimming, jogging and sailing. My favourite activity is cooking. I really love it. I work in my brother's restaurant at the weekends.

Do you like sport? Do you like cooking?

Write and tell me about yourself. Your friend, John

Pronunciation
2

/æ/	/ɑː/
animal	apartment
band	aunt
chat	car
family	dancing
handbag	father
have	large
man	partner

5 Days

Grammar
1

2) does 3) has 4) works
5) has 6) reads 7) have
8) watch 9) go

2

b) It's four forty-five. / It's quarter to five.
c) It's twelve thirty. / It's half past twelve.
d) It's two ten. / It's ten past two.
e) It's six twenty. / It's twenty past six.
f) It's eight forty. / It's twenty to nine.
g) It's one fifty-five. / It's five to two.
h) It's three thirty-five. / It's twenty-five to four.

3

b) What time do you have breakfast?
c) What time do you go to work?
d) What time do you have dinner?
e) What time do you go to bed?

Vocabulary
1

Monday	**F**riday
Tuesday	**Sa**turday
Wednesday	**S**unday
Thursday	

2

2 it 3 receipt 4 Thank
5 is 6 please 7 Can

3

have	go
breakfast	to bed
dinner	home
a good time	on the internet
lunch	out
a shower	shopping
	to work

4

2 have breakfast
3 go to work
4 have lunch
5 go home
6 have dinner
7 go on the internet
8 go to bed
9 go shopping
10 go out
11 have a good time

Listening
1

a) Alana b) Toby

2

a) La Cucina b) in c) friends
d) eggs e) friend f) Luc
g) dancing

3

2 city centre (Sydney)
3 clothes
4 Italian
5 beach
6 (my) friends
7 listen to music
8 shopping
9 (my) friend (Makiko)
10 Japanese
11 cinema
12 (my) sister
13 French

Pronunciation
1

2 A: You live in New Orleans.
   B: No, I live in New <u>York</u>.

2

b) No, I like swimming and <u>tennis</u>.
c) No, I'm a <u>taxi</u> driver.
d) No, my <u>mother</u>'s a lawyer.
e) No, I have <u>dinner</u> at home.
f) No, I love eating in <u>Italian</u> restaurants.

Writing
1

2 After 3 After 4 Then

2

a) Then b) After

3

2 shopping 3 museum
4 National Theatre 5 Swan Lake
6 ballet

6 Living

Grammar
1

b) I live in the city.
c) My parents drive a Porsche.
d) Our teacher gives us homework.
e) I do the housework.
f) My father drinks a lot of tea.
g) My family has breakfast together.

2

b) I don't live in the city.
c) My parents don't drive a Porsche.
d) Our teacher doesn't give us homework.
e) I don't do the housework.
f) My father doesn't drink a lot of tea.
g) My family doesn't have breakfast together.

4

b) Ali's hardly ever late for class.
c) I always train at the weekend.
d) They're never open on Sunday.
e) Do you ever go to bed after midnight?
f) She's usually at work until 7.30 p.m.

5

15th May	January	night
Sunday	the evening	seven o'clock
Tuesday morning	the spring	the weekend

6

2 in 3 On 4 In 5 at 6 in
7 in 8 On 9 At

Vocabulary

1

Northern hemisphere

Spring	Summer	Autumn	Winter
March	June	September	December
April	July	October	January
May	August	November	February

Southern hemisphere

Spring	Summer	Autumn	Winter
September	December	March	June
October	January	April	July
November	February	May	August

2

b) do   c) make   d) do   e) does
f) making   g) doing   h) make

4

b) We write: 15th March
   We say: the fifteenth of March
c) We write: 1st June
   We say: the first of June
d) We write: 28th November
   We say: the twenty-eighth of November.
e) We write: 31st December
   We say: the thirty-first of December

5

2 closed   3 closes   4 time
5 open   6 opens

Listening

1

fun, school, costumes, parade, party, food, sweets

2

b) F   (It's on 31st October.)
c) F   d) F (Her sister was a rabbit.)
e) T   f) F
g) F   (They go to bed really late.)

3

b) They watch the parade.
c) They play games and eat special Halloween food.
d) They go to a street party (in Perry Avenue).
e) They wear (funny) costumes.
f) People give the children sweets.

Pronunciation

2

/z/	/s/	/ɪz/
drives	drinks	finishes
goes	likes	teaches
has	starts	watches
listens	takes	
lives	visits	

Writing

1 b) 3   c) 2   d) 1

7 Sea

Grammar

1

b) phoned   c) loved   d) wanted
e) played   f) worked   g) studied
h) watched   i) started   j) stopped

2

b) watched   c) phoned   d) started
e) wanted   f) played

3

break	broke
come	came
do	did
have	had
say	said
see	saw
sell	sold
sit	sat
take	took

4

b) When was the last time you read a good book?
c) When was the last time you wore blue?
d) When was the last time you lost something?

6

2 studied   3 wanted   4 could
5 made   6 sailed   7 had
8 watched   9 listened   10 made
11 saw   12 took

Vocabulary

1

b) swimming   c) sailing
d) scuba diving   e) surfing
f) fishing   g) kite surfing

2

b) last week / a week ago
c) last year / a year ago
d) six months ago
e) yesterday

3

2 At first   3 After   4 Suddenly
5 later   6 eventually

4

In Paris it's rainy.
In Rio de Janeiro it's sunny.
In Madrid it's windy.
In Bangkok it's cloudy.
In New York it's snowy.

Reading

1 Picture b

2

b) to the beach   c) reading
d) stayed near   e) sharks
f) the beach

3

b) It was hot and sunny.
c) They went to sleep.
d) A man.
e) Terrified.
f) He stayed on the beach (with his mother).

Pronunciation

2

/d/	/t/	/ɪd/
called	asked	needed
listened	finished	repeated
lived	liked	shouted
loved	stopped	started
played	talked	waited
used	watched	wanted

Writing

1 2 d   3 b   4 a

2

In 2006, Eve and Sebastian Rankin went to Sicily on holiday.

One day, Eve and Sebastian decided to go windsurfing for the first time.

At first, they did well and enjoyed themselves.

After an hour, the weather got cold and windy.

Suddenly, the wind took Sebastian and his windsurfing board out to sea. Sebastian was terrified and Eve was very worried.

Five minutes later, a boat went out to find Sebastian.

Eventually the boat returned, with Sebastian.

8 Alone

Grammar

1

b) I went to school.
c) I lived in a different city.
d) I worked at the weekend.
e) I listened to rock music.
f) I enjoyed my life.

2

b) Did you go to school?
c) Did you live in a different city?
d) Did you work at the weekend?
e) Did you listen to rock music?
f) Did you enjoy your life?

4

2 lost   3 left   4 got   5 moved
6 started   7 had   8 became
9 stopped   10 died

5

b) When was he born?
c) Where did he grow up?
d) What did he do? / What was his job?
e) Did he have any children?
f) When did he die?

Vocabulary

1

a) angry   b) interested
c) excited   d) embarrassed
e) nervous   f) frightened   g) sad
h) bored

2

2 about   3 of   4 with   5 in
6 about

3

2 Let's   3 Why don't you
4 Let's   5 let's   6 Why don't you

Reading

1

She's a sailor. / She sails.

2

a) 3   b) 6   c) 1   d) 5   e) 2
f) 4

3

b) F   c) F   d) T   e) T   f) F
g) T   h) F

Pronunciation

1

Speaker A sounds bored. Speaker B sounds interested.

Writing

1

b) last month
c) her friends (Frank and Cassie)
d) by plane/air
e) in a small hotel
f) went to good restaurants, swam with dolphins
g) whales

2

b) great   c) beautiful
d) really nice, small   e) friendly
f) good

9 Hotel

Grammar

1

b) There are   c) There are
d) There's   e) There are
f) There's   g) There are
h) There are

2

b) any   c) some   d) any
e) a   f) some

3

b) Is there a mirror in the living room?
c) Are there any cupboards in the kitchen?
d) Is there a book on the table?
e) Are there any cushions on the sofa?
f) Is there a cooker in the kitchen?
g) Are there any plants in the kitchen?
h) Are there any plants in the living room?

4

b) Yes, there is.
c) Yes, there are.
d) No, there isn't.
e) No, there aren't.
f) Yes, there is.
g) No, there aren't.
h) Yes, there are.

Vocabulary

1

1 sitting room
a) curtains   b) plant   c) sofa
d) coffee table   e) armchair
f) bookcase   g) rug   h) desk
2 kitchen
i) cupboard   j) cooker   k) fridge
3 bathroom
l) shower   m) mirror
n) washbasin   o) bath
4 bedroom
p) lamp   q) cushion   r) carpet

2

b) on   c) under   d) above
e) next to   f) in the corner

3

b) in   c) near   d) in   e) near
f) on

4

2 help   3 have a problem
4 What's   5 work   6 I'll send

Listening

1

b) phone   c) balcony
d) washing machine   e) TV
f) fridge   g) shower   h) plants

2 a), c), d), f) and g)

3

b) small   c) sea   d) TV
e) city   f) The concierge

4

b) F   c) T   d) F   e) F   f) T

Writing

1

The note answers questions a), d), e), f) and g).

Pronunciation

2

/s/	/ʃ/
centre	chandelier
paradise	cushions
peace	shampoo
place	shower
seaplane	spacious
stress	special
suite	washbasin

10 Food

Grammar

1

Countable nouns	Uncountable nouns
potato	bread
mushroom	cheese
grape	olive oil
orange	cereal
carrot	garlic

2

2 some   3 any   4 a   5 a   6 a
7 any   8 some   9 any   10 any

3

2 are   3 is   4 isn't   5 Are
6 aren't   7 Is   8 is

4

b) much   c) many   d) much
e) much   f) many

5

2 c   3 f   4 b   5 e   6 a

Vocabulary

1

Across		Down	
2	oranges	1	pasta
3	carrots	3	cauliflower
6	fish	4	rice
7	tomatoes	5	apples
8	melon	9	onions
13	potatoes	10	cheese
14	eggs	11	bananas
15	meat	12	bread

2

Carbohydrate	Protein	Vegetable	Fruit
pasta	cheese	cauliflower	apples
rice	fish	onions	bananas
bread	eggs	carrots	oranges
potatoes	meat	tomatoes	melon

3 b) garlic   c) pears   d) pasta

4

2 Would   3 brown   4 you
5 anything   6 black   7 That's

Reading

1

the Greek island of Crete

2

b) has a lot of   c) good
d) with their food   e) sugar
f) different types of food

3

b) F   c) T   d) F   e) T   f) F
g) T

Pronunciation

2

/ɪ/	/iː/
chicken	beans
chips	cheese
different	eat
fish	meat
garlic	need
list	protein
live	seafood

Writing

1

Invitation 1 is written in a formal style.

Invitation 2 is written in an informal style.

2

a) Invitation 2: lunch
b) Invitation 1: James Gregg
   Invitation 2: Kristy
c) Invitation 1: Riverside House,
   the Ridings, Sprotton
   Invitation 2: at Kristy's flat, Flat 2,
   Park Villas, Gadd Street
d) Invitation 1: Friday 14th July
   Invitation 2: on Sunday
e) Invitation 1: 9pm
   Invitation 2: 12 o'clock
f) Invitation 1: RSVP
   Invitation 2: Call me this week!

11 Looks

Grammar

1

b) 's wearing   c) 'm sitting
d) 're singing   e) 're making
f) 're working

2

b) Is it raining?
c) Are your friends making a noise
   outside?
d) Am I standing on your foot?
e) Are we earning a lot of money?
f) Is she wearing a black top?

3

b) No, it isn't.   c) Yes, they are.
d) No, you aren't.   e) Yes, we are.
f) No, she isn't.

4

b) What are you wearing?
c) Where are you sitting?
d) Are you drinking a cup of coffee?
e) Are you having a good time?

Vocabulary

1 and 2

b) skirt – S
c) jacket – S
d) trousers – P
e) shoes – P
f) boots – P
g) tie – S
h) trainers – P
i) T-shirt – S
j) shirt – S
k) jeans – P
l) sweater – S
m) suit – S
n) hat – S
o) top – S
p) sunglasses – P

3

Footwear: boots, shoes, trainers

Formal clothes: skirt, top, trousers, shirt, tie, suit

Casual clothes: T-shirt, jeans, sweater, jacket

Accessories: belt, hat, sunglasses

4

2 blond   3 eyes   4 beard
5 good-looking   6 lovely smile
7 sweet   8 medium-length
9 straight   10 brown

5

2 looking   3 special   4 colour
5 about   6 have   7 try
8 changing rooms

Listening

1 c) didn't happen

2

b) pink top   c) after   d) the fans
e) earrings   f) trainers

3 b) F   c) T   d) T   e) F   f) T

Pronunciation

2

a) 30   b) 14   c) 15   d) 60
e) 17   f) 80   g) 19

Writing

1

a) five   b) two   c) *with*
d) *and*   e) *and*

2

2 He has short, black hair.
3 He has brown eyes.
4 He has a moustache and a beard.
5 He's wearing casual/black clothes.
6 He's handsome/good-looking.

3

Orlando Bloom is a young man with short, black hair and brown eyes. He has a moustache and a beard and he's wearing casual/black clothes. He's handsome/good-looking.

12 Money

Grammar

1

Short adjectives	Comparative form
clean	cleaner
fast	faster
old	older
tall	taller
cheap	cheaper
short	shorter
young	younger
ugly	uglier

Long adjectives	
beautiful	more beautiful
interesting	more interesting
expensive	more expensive
famous	more famous

Irregular	
good	better
bad	worse
far	further

2

b) younger   c) more expensive
d) cheaper   e) more beautiful
f) uglier   g) better   h) worse

3

b) The most expensive
c) the most important
d) the best
e) the happiest
f) the biggest

4

b) the tallest
c) the youngest
d) the oldest
e) the most valuable
f) the most famous

Vocabulary

1

b) buy   c) earn   d) spend
e) debt   f) salary   g) bills
h) credit

2

2 salary   3 earn   4 spend
5 bills   6 save   7 buy   8 credit

3

b) seven hundred and twenty-four thousand, one hundred and fifteen dollars

c) four hundred and ninety-nine thousand, one hundred and thirty dollars

d) thirteen million, one hundred and ninety-four thousand, seven hundred and twenty dollars

4

b) $12,785,220   c) $78,290

d) $1,145,859   e) $819,440

f) $212,350

5

2 handbag   3 anything   4 brown
5 leather   6 good

Reading

1 b)

2

b) transport   c) 46 / forty-six
d) free-time activities
e) more   f) other

3

b) F They lived in the USA.
c) T   d) F They are smaller.
e) F They spend more.   f) T

Pronunciation

b) de<u>b</u>t   c) <u>wr</u>ote
d) han<u>d</u>some   e) cu<u>p</u>board
f) int<u>e</u>resting   g) diff<u>e</u>rent
h) t<u>w</u>o

Writing

1

2 spends most on
3 The second highest thing is
4 After that
5 A surprising thing is
6 spends more on

2

b) housing and electricity
c) transport
d) *students' own answer*

13 Talent

Grammar

1

b) He can't drive. e) It can talk.
c) We can ski.   f) You can walk.
d) I can swim.

2

b) Can your teacher speak Italian?
c) Can you cook?
d) Can your parents ski?
e) Can you sing?
f) Can you and your friends dance?

4

Adjective	Adverb
bad	badly
good	well
careful	carefully
happy	happily
fast	fast
loud	loudly
quiet	quietly
slow	slowly

5

b) Isabella talks very fast.
c) My sister sings really well.
d) Ken does his work carefully.
e) They talk very loudly.
f) I swim very badly.

6

Frequent   all the time
                           twice a day
                           every day
                           once a month
                           every year
Not frequent   never

Vocabulary

1

b) generous   c) selfish
d) sensible   e) serious   f) shy

2

b) shy   c) sensible   d) selfish
e) serious   f) confident

3

b) unfriendly   c) serious
d) stupid   e) quiet

4

2 have   3 about   4 money
5 can't   6 tired   7 bad   8 time

Reading

1

a) Keith Richards   b) Ronnie Wood
c) Johnny Depp

2 b) T   c) F   d) F   e) T   f) T

3

2 thirteen   3 musical instruments
4 music   5 Keith Richards
6 Depp's   7 Ronnie Wood

Writing

1

2 CD   3 Rome   4 Italy
5 Italian

2

2 school (line 2)   3 guitar (line 3)
4 year (line 4)   5 every (line 7)
6 summer (line 8)   7 week (line 9)
8 really (line 12)

3

a) Paragraph 4   b) Paragraph 1
c) Paragraph 2   d) Paragraph 3

14 TV

Grammar

1

b) When do you hope to retire?
c) Would you like to be famous?
d) Do you want to get married?
e) Do you want to live in a foreign country?
f) Would you like to travel round the world?

2 2 c   3 b   4 a   5 f   6 d

3

b) What are you going to buy tomorrow?
c) What are you going to watch on TV tonight?
d) Who are you going to see next weekend?
e) Where are you going to go for your next holiday?
f) Who are you going to meet tomorrow?

5

b) 's   c) don't   d) 'd   e) to
f) not   g) 're

Vocabulary

1

a) chat show   b) documentary
c) game show   d) the news
e) reality TV show   f) soap opera

2

2 soap opera   3 reality TV show
4 game show   5 the news
6 documentary

3

2 programme   3 switch   4 watch
5 on   6 channels

4

2 tired   3 stay   4 watch   5 on
6 Shall   7 Let's   8 I'll   9 choose

Listening

1

Lucy is Darren Brown's dog.

2 b) T   c) F   d) F   e) T   f) F

3

b) No, he doesn't.
c) Yes, she does.
d) No, it isn't. (It's small.)
e) the old dogs' home
f) a new bicycle

Pronunciation

2

/ɒ/	/əʊ/
lots	clothes
opera	don't
pop	home
stop	hope
want	show
watch	soap

Writing

1 The three reasons are a, c and d.

2 a) because   b) and   c) but

3 a) because   b) and   c) but

15 Experiences

Grammar

1

b) Clara has been to Paris.
c) They haven't been to Japan.
d) Dan has been to over 30 countries.
e) My parents have been to Spain six times.
f) I haven't been to Berlin.
g) We have been to Hong Kong twice.

2

b) 's/has swum
c) 's/has driven
d) have worked
e) 've/have met
f) have sailed
g) 've/have seen

3

b) went   c) has seen
d) haven't been   e) met
f) bought

4

b) Have you ever seen someone famous?
c) Have you ever lost something valuable?
d) Have you ever read a book in one day?
e) Have you ever flown in a small plane?

Vocabulary

1

b) done   c) driven   d) flown
e) said   f) swum   g) won
h) worked

2

a) met; spoken   b) seen
c) bought   d) read   e) had
f) known   g) broken   h) lost
i) given

3

2 Smoking   3 something   4 have
5 ready   6 like   7 Would
8 menu   9 everything   10 bill

Reading

1 a), b) and d) are mentioned.

2

b) the sea   c) women   d) liked
e) river   f) are

3

b) T   c) F   d) T   e) F   f) F
g) F

Writing

1

a) i) What's the best place you've ever visited?
   ii) What's the most unusual food you've ever eaten?
b) Morro de Sao Paulo, Brazil
c) snake

2

b) Where   c) How   d) When
e) Would   f) How   g) When
h) What   i) Would

3

Questions a), b), c), d), g), h), i) were answered.

Questions e) and f) were not answered.

Pronunciation

1

b) hurt   c) said   d) been

2

a) won   done   run   *swum*
b) caught   bought   taught   *thought*
c) played   made   paid   *shaken*
d) slept   met   meant   *read*

16 Drive

Grammar

1

b) about   c) to   d) with   e) to
f) for

3

a) have   b) 's waiting
c) don't like   d) 'm watching
e) 'm driving   f) takes

4

b) Did you have   c) 've seen
d) went   e) wrote   f) have won

5

2 has been   3 is going to visit
4 flies   5 travels   6 's getting
7 has had   8 broke   9 spent
10 's going to start   11 wants

Vocabulary

1

Across		Down	
4	waterfall	1	sand
5	bridge	2	desert
6	forest	3	cliff
8	beach	7	rocks
9	grass	10	snow
12	mountain	11	hills
13	trees		

2

b) out of   c) across   d) along
e) past   f) up   g) over   h) into

3

2 turning   3 end   4 turn
5 straight   6 on   7 opposite

Listening

1

a) Highway 1 – photo 2
b) Picos de Europa – photo 1
c) Route 62 – photo 3

2

b) P (Picos de Europa)
c) R (Route 62)
d) P (Picos de Europa)
e) H (Highway 1)
f) R (Route 62)

3

b) three days
c) horses
d) his family
e) the N2 – the Garden Route
f) a green valley with trees and wild flowers

Writing

1

2 busy   3 quieter   4 mountains
5 lakes   6 600   7 3

2

b) old   c) terrible   d) spectacular
e) beautiful   f) fantastic

Pronunciation

b) The <u>traffic</u> is <u>terrible</u>.
c) My <u>car</u> is so <u>old</u>.
d) What <u>beautiful</u> <u>shoes</u>!
e) This <u>weather</u> is <u>fantastic</u>.
f) The <u>views</u> were <u>amazing</u>.